The Embedded Librarian's Cookbook

edited by Kaijsa Calkins and Cassandra Kvenild

D0731514

Association of College and Research Libraries
A division of the American Library Association
Chicago 2014

The paper used in this publication meets the minimum requirements of American National Standard for Information Sciences-Permanence of Paper for Printed Library Materials, ANSI Z39.48-1992. ∞

The ACRL Cookbook series was conceived of and designed by Ryan Sittler and Doug Cook. Other books in this series:

The Library Instruction Cookbook by Ryan L. Sittler and Douglas Cook

Library of Congress Cataloging-in-Publication Data

The embedded librarian's cookbook / edited by Kaijsa Calkins and Cassandra Kvenild.
    pages cm
  Includes bibliographical references and index.
  ISBN 978-0-8389-8693-6 (pbk. : alk. paper) 1. Academic libraries--Relations with faculty and curriculum. 2. Information literacy--Study and teaching (Higher) 3. Research--Methodology--Study and teaching (Higher) 4. Library orientation for college students. I. Calkins, Kaijsa, editor of compilation. II. Kvenild, Cassandra, editor of compilation.
  Z675.U5E446 2014
  025.5'677--dc23
                              2014017061

Printed in the United States of America.

18 17 16 15 14   5 4 3 2 1

TABLE OF CONTENTS

Acknowledgements

This book has been on our minds and in our hearts since 2009. It is the product of the confluence of several events and the generosity of many people.

When writing the proposal for our first book, *Embedded Librarians: Moving Beyond One-shot Instruction*, there were no book-length treatments of embedded librarianship. It was clear that librarians were interested in learning more about how to successfully embed instruction and other library services into the working lives of their communities. The response to our call for chapter proposals for that book proved to be nearly overwhelming, and we immediately considered publishing a second volume. At the same time, the excellent *Library Instruction Cookbook* from Ryan L. Sittler and Douglas Cook debuted and seemed to scratch an itch many instruction librarians had, including us. And thus, Cass had the great idea to propose a cookbook for embedded librarians.

We are grateful to Sittler and Cook for inspiring us with their original cookbook and for agreeing to help build a series patterned on their book (and for letting us be a part of that series). Thanks to Kathryn Deiss of ACRL for connecting us all together, for greenlighting the book, and for being the most patient, encouraging, and generally awesome editor around. We are also thankful to Dawn Mueller at ACRL for her copyediting prowess and for her beautiful layout of the book.

We would also like to acknowledge our peers who are publishing excellent works on embedded librarianship, especially David Shumaker, Beth Tumbleson and John Burke, and Elizabeth Leonard and Erin McCaffrey. It is a privilege to know and collaborate with fellow authors in the congenial and generous field of embedded librarianship. Thank you for your support and inspiration.

Utmost thanks to all of the cookbook authors who shared their excellence with us in these pages. Their recipes are full of ideas that have been kitchen-tested by experienced librarians. Each of their contributions can be implemented in a variety of libraries to benefit students, faculty, and the academic community. We learned something new and interesting from every recipe in this book.

We extend gratitude to our work family of amazing faculty, staff and administration at the University of Wyoming, as well as to our families at home. Thanks for your continued support and enthusiasm for our work.

HOW TO CONTACT US
Kaijsa Calkins
University of Wyoming Libraries
kcalkins@uwyo.edu

Cass Kvenild
University of Wyoming Libraries
ckvenild@uwyo.edu

How to Use This Book

This cookbook is separated into two main parts. Part I contains six sections bursting with hands-on recipes for embedded instruction, all written by experienced librarians eager to share their successful projects:

- Section 1: Amuse Bouche: Bite Sized Embedded Projects
- Section 2: First Courses: Embedding in the First-Year Experience
- Section 3: Everyday Meals: Adaptable Instructions for Embedded Projects
- Section 4: Regional Cuisine: Embedding in the Disciplines
- Section 5: Al Fresco Dining: Embedding in Online Courses
- Section 6: Tailgating: Embedding Outside of the Library and Outside of the Classroom

Part II contains two sections designed for mature embedded programs and librarians looking to build a space for embedded instruction in their long-range planning. The authors give insight into creating scalable embedded programs and assessing the impact of embedded library instruction:

- Section 1: Test Kitchen: Assessing Your Efforts
- Section 2: Menu Planning: Creating a Long Term Plan for Embedded Instruction

Each recipe that appears in the book is broken down into the sections described below. We hope that the recipe layout will make the book easy to skim, so that you may quickly select and implement the right projects for you.

Nutrition information offers a quick summary of the project and includes some background information.

Serves indicates how many students can be accommodated by the embedded project. As with traditional recipes, many of these projects can be adapted to serve larger or smaller groups.

Cooking time offers an estimate of the time required for the project. If you're looking for a new approach to embedded librarianship, it is crucial to plan ahead to avoid overloading yourself with an unsustainable project. These guidelines can help you set reasonable time and workload expectations for yourself, your collaborators, and other members of your instructional team.

It is always important to know what **Ingredients and equipment** you will need before you get started on a new project. While the authors list specific technologies that worked for them, feel free to look for equivalents and substitutions that are available in your institution.

Preparation provides a guide to your mise en place, or what work you need to do before the instructional part of a project begins.

The meat of the recipe is the **Cooking method** section. Here you'll find the directions for making your project work.

Allergy warnings are useful cautions from the authors, based on their experiences preparing the recipe over time.

Chef's notes are personalized from recipe to recipe. Some authors discuss the enhanced collaboration or stronger relationships they built through their projects, while others relate the most successful parts of the instruction they provided.

Additional resources appear in some of the recipes, in the form of guides and pointers to articles that may be of assistance in developing similar projects.

1. Amuse Bouche: Bite Sized Embedded Projects

In this section, librarians share their favorite bite-sized embedded projects. The projects are small in scale, allowing you to try out embedding without making a major commitment across a discipline or signing on for a research project that extends over several weeks.

When piloting an embedded library instruction program, short-term projects such as these are an excellent way to gauge interest in embedded instruction as well as staff time required.

How to Create an Embedded Library Instruction Services (ELIS) Assignment

SaraJane Tompkins, Associate Professor in Academic Information Services, Olson Library, stompkin@nmu.edu; Michael F. Strahan, Associate Professor in Academic Information Services, Olson Library, mstrahan@nmu.edu; Judith Puncochar, Associate Professor of Educational Psychology, School of Education, Leadership, & Public Service, jpuncoch@nmu.edu, Northern Michigan University

NUTRITION INFORMATION

Assessment of Student Learning and Functionality of Embedded Project in Online Courses

SERVES

Typically 25, but can be adjusted for larger or smaller crowds

COOKING TIME

- Librarian: 1 hour for preparation of ELIS into course content
- Instructor: 2 hours (includes one hour of assignment preparation and one hour to assess student work)
- Students: 1 hour of homework
- Continuous Quality Improvement—½ hour of instructor time plus ½ hour of librarian time to evaluate student responses and implement any revisions to ELIS, the assignment, and/or instruction based on student responses.

INFORMATION DIETARY STANDARDS ADDRESSED

ACRL Information Literacy Standards for Teacher Education (http://www.ala.org/acrl/sites/ala.org.acrl/files/content/standards/ilstandards_te.pdf)

Standard 2: The information literate teacher education student locates and selects information based on its appropriateness to the specific information need and the developmental needs of the student.

Performance Indicator: *Locates information.*

Outcomes

- The student employs proper terminology by translating concepts into accurate keywords and synonyms by using provided tools, such as controlled vocabularies, thesauruses, or indexes. Example: Student keeps a record of search terms, including keywords and descriptors from the *Thesaurus of ERIC Descriptors,* Library of Congress Authorities, or other subject headings.
- The student revises searches based on results.
- The student employs linkages among documents to identify additional pertinent information. Example: Student follows cited references or hyperlinks.
- The student employs specialized online ELIS services, such as interlibrary loan, library distance education services, virtual reference services and guides, an embedded librarian, and library search engines.

Standard 6: The information literate teacher education student knows how to ethically use and disseminate information.

Performance Indicator: *Ethically uses and disseminates information.*

Outcome

- The student is able to select and use an appropriate documentation using the *Publication Manual of the American Psychological Association* (APA) style to cite or give credit to original information sources.

INGREDIENTS AND EQUIPMENT

- 1 Instructor
- 1 Librarian
- 1 Online Course Management System (e.g., Moodle)
- 1 to 25 or more students with online access
- 1 Library Block Content known as Embedded Library Instruction Services (ELIS) for student access to the embedded librarian
- 1 ELIS Assignment

PREPARATION

The instructor creates an assignment to assess students' understanding of the usefulness of ELIS to find research articles. The instructor assesses students' proper application of APA style to cite and reference information sources (see Figure 1).

COOKING METHOD

Library Block Contents

1. Discovery resource (OneSearch) search box
2. Other course-specific databases
3. How-to videos
4. Course-specific library guide
5. Other library guides (e.g., theses & dissertations)
6. Course-specific library resources and services (e.g., *Cabell's*)
7. Citing/referencing style library guide (APA, MLA, Chicago/Turabian, etc.)
8. Contact information / methods of access to embedded liaison person (including chat box)

FIGURE 1. Example of ELIS content embedded into an online course management system

PROVIDE DIRECTIONS
Directions to Students

Read about ELIS resources by accessing the ELIS blocks on the right-hand side of Moodle. Write a statement indicating you have explored ELIS tools, the library's APA guide, and DOI (Digital Object Identifier) information. Using the customized OneSearch search box in ELIS, find a research article with a title of interest to you. Create a document with the following items:

1. The research article's title;
2. A list of the search word(s) and phrase(s) used to find the research article;
3. Include the DOI, or the journal home page web address when no DOI is assigned;
4. Create an APA style reference appropriate for the research article;
5. Write your ELIS reflections, which include your overall impressions, usefulness for locating research articles, and suggestions for improvement; and,
6. Upload your document to the Moodle assignment box.

Thank you!

FIGURE 2. Customized search widget with librarian-recommended resources

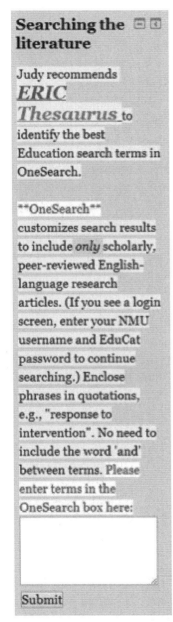

Directions to Librarians

1. Obtain instructor's permission for library presence in the Moodle course
2. Build Library Block Content in the course
3. Create a Library Discussion Forum in the course

Directions to Instructors

1. Align ELIS Assignment with syllabus course goals and learning outcomes
2. Prepare ELIS assessment matrix (see Figure 1)
3. Set an ELIS due date, usually within the first two weeks of class
4. Score students' work with the ELIS matrix
5. Compile students' reflections of overall impressions of ELIS
6. Use student reflections to improve ELIS, course content, and instruction.

The purpose of an ELIS Assignment is to introduce students to basic research techniques and skills necessary to make informed judgments about the utility and validity of educational research. Students engage in the process of finding, reading, interpreting, analyzing, evaluating, and summarizing research articles in APA style.

GOAL 1—KNOWLEDGE—Objective: To interpret research results and present findings on an approved topic for a literature review. OUTCOME—Students complete a search to find quality research article(s). The submitted assignment is assessed using the ELIS Grading Matrix.

GOAL 2—REFLECTION—Objective: Students analyze, evaluate, and reflect on the effectiveness and quality of their work and are open to new ideas. OUTCOME—Students provide feedback on ELIS impressions, usefulness for locating research articles, and suggestions for improvement.

ALLERGY WARNINGS

The instructor should decide whether to allow references to dissertations, theses, and/or non-peer reviewed publications.

CHEF'S NOTE

Using ELIS resources and services, students should be able to develop a systematic procedure to find online peer-reviewed research articles on an approved topic to write a literature review. The process of writing a literature review is an attempt "to establish that the writer has a thorough command of the literature on the topic being studied" (Galvan, 2013, p. 13).

ADDITIONAL RESOURCES

- "Information Literacy Standards for Teacher Education," EBSS Instruction for Educators Committee, Association of College and Research Libraries, approved May 11, 2011, http://crln.acrl.org/content/72/7/420.full.
- "ELIS - Embedded Library Instruction Services Request Form," Northern Michigan University, Lydia M. Olson

Library, last modified August 25, 2013, accessed November 11, 2013, http://library.nmu.edu/forms/mailerforms/elis_request.php.

- American Psychological Association, *Publication Manual of the American Psychological Association,* 6th ed. (Washington, DC: Author, 2009).
- "APA Reference Style Guide," Northern Michigan University, Lydia M. Olson Library, last modified October 21, 2013, accessed November 11, 2013, http://library.nmu.edu/guides/userguides/style_apa.htm.
- "How to use OneSearch" Video, 4:53, Northern Michigan University, Lydia M. Olson Library, last modified June 25, 2011, accessed November 11, 2013, http://library.nmu.edu/redirects/one-searched500.htm.
- Jose L. Galvan, *Writing Literature Reviews: A Guide for Students of the Social and Behavioral Sciences,* 5th ed. (Glendale, CA: Pyrczak, 2013).

Just Because It's on Google Doesn't Mean It's Free for Me to Use!
Helping Students Navigate the Muddy Waters of Copyright and Fair Use!

Michelle Costello, Education and Instructional Design Librarian, SUNY Geneseo, costello@geneseo.edu; Maria Perpetua Socorro U. Liwanag, Assistant Professor, Towson University, liwanag@geneseo.edu; Steve Dresbach, Technology Instructor, Milne Library, SUNY Geneseo, dresbach@geneseo.edu

NUTRITION INFORMATION
This recipe is designed as a demo of image and music websites and an introduction to copyright, and fair use issues as undergraduate education students prepare to create book trailers for a class project. The book trailer assignment is designed to highlight and promote a young adult book students are reading and analyzing in class. Through the book trailer project, students are able to engage in what it means to read, write, and create using multiple literacies.

The purpose is to introduce students to the concepts of copyright, fair use and the public domain in order to help them ethically find, access, and cite images and music for their book trailer assignment (and ultimately future digital projects).

SERVES
20–30 students

COOKING TIME
50–60 minutes plus optional 50–60 minute hands-on follow-up workshop

INGREDIENTS AND EQUIPMENT
- Computer access for all students
- Instructor's station
- Handout

PREPARATION
A guide should be created for students in the class. The guide would contain information about copyright and book trailers and how to create them (including videos). It would also include links to websites for finding images and music for digital projects (such as book trailers).

Prior to the session students will have picked a young adult book and received instruction from their professor on finding images and music that best represent the text and themes of their book.

COOKING METHOD
Part One: View presentation on copyright, public domain and creative commons with a follow-up discussion
Students view a Prezi presentation[1] which includes a YouTube video on copyright, public domain, and fair use (Fair[y] Use Tale[2]). After viewing the video, students are asked to define each of the concepts and point out the differences. The Prezi presentation also includes a few tips on how to legally and ethically find images and music for digital projects including; creating your own content, gaining permission of the copyright holder, and finding content that is either in the public domain or under a creative commons license. The need to cite their sources is also introduced at this point.

Part Two: Instructor demonstration
Students are shown the library guide which contains links to the Prezi presentation, the Fair(y) Use Tale video, information about copyright and book trailers and a plethora of links to sites for finding images and music for their projects. Make sure to point out where they can find the various content and contact information for follow-up questions. After a quick introduction to the guide, choose a sample theme or topic from a young adult book (or ask students for one of their themes) and perform a few searches highlighting a couple of music and image sites. Bring up the idea of citing their sources again and mention that they will receive more information about how to cite later in the session.

Part Three: Individual and/or group searching

Let students explore the various sites and try some searches on their own (or with their group). Walk around the room and make sure that students are finding material and that they know how to save what they find to their own laptops (or flash drive if working on a lab computer). Let students know that they will receive instruction from the technology specialist on how to add the music and images to their book trailers at a subsequent session. Students will consider elements of the story that represent their understanding through the images and music they select.

Part Four: Handout on citation styles

Explain to students that detailed instruction on how to cite their sources will not be covered during this session; however they should practice on their own using the given handout on citing images and music and set up one-on-one appointments with a librarian to go over their citations and ask questions. In addition, a separate workshop can be scheduled to give students time to practice citing and to work on their book trailers with help from the instruction librarian, faculty member, and technology instructor.

ALLERGY WARNING

Students are used to grabbing images and music from the Internet or from CDs/iPods without thinking about copyright issues which could lead to some initial resistance and confusion on their part. By explaining copyright to them in easy to understand terms it decreases their anxiety and educates them on a very important issue. Additionally finding quality images and music that do not violate copyright law can be challenging and this may frustrate students. Having an arsenal of good websites available as well as giving students a clear understanding of what creative commons licenses are (and how helpful they can be) sets them up for success rather than failure. Students are also unsure of when and how to cite so giving them examples (from handouts or library guides) is essential.

CHEFS' NOTE

This session works best if it is part of a collaboration between the faculty member, an instruction librarian, and a technology instructor. In order to produce quality digital projects students need to be educated on three fronts; learning the technology needed to produce the projects (technology instructor), grasping copyright law and how to choose material in an ethical manner (librarian), and understanding the goals/objectives of the digital project itself (faculty member). The session should ideally take place after the faculty member's introduction of the digital project and before the technology workshop on software applications, so students know what content to look for and how to legally find that material before learning how to use the technology to create their projects.

NOTES

1. http://prezi.com/4kbj1ixae3h0/copy-right-and-digital-projects/
2. http://cyberlaw.stanford.edu/blog/2007/03/fairy-use-tale

INSTRUCTIONAL RESOURCES

- http://libguides.geneseo.edu/curr313

Tapas-style Instruction:
Small Bytes for Speech/Debate Campers

Michelle Twait, Academic Librarian and Associate Professor, Gustavus Adolphus College, St. Peter, MN, mtwait@gustavus.edu

NUTRITION INFORMATION

Middle school and high school students attending a week-long summer speech camp on a college campus are expected to quickly select materials to use as part of an interpretive performance of a literary piece or an informative/persuasive speech. In most cases, students have never used a college library, are unfamiliar with the Library of Congress classification system, and are under pressure to identify resources within the first 24–48 hours of the camp. College librarians offer instruction sessions and provide reference support during the week. This recipe highlights the topics covered during the instruction session and the activities used to introduce students to the library and its resources.

In addition to familiarizing students with the library's layout and the materials available, the session helps students identify and narrow topics, then select appropriate search tools and strategies.

SERVES

20–30 hungry students

COOKING TIME

50 minutes plus ongoing support throughout the week

INGREDIENTS AND EQUIPMENT

- Computer access for all students
- Instructor's station
- Whiteboard/blackboard
- Sample reference works
- Several tables displaying books, each table highlighting titles for a certain event category (e.g. poetry, great speeches, humor, etc.)

PREPARATION

Preparation for the speech camp begins months before the campers arrive. The librarian works closely with the Director of Summer Academic Programs and coaches to determine the schedule and format for the library sessions. The librarian also works with them to identify any collection development needs (i.e. new plays, poetry books, short story anthologies, etc.). The coaches are also able to provide helpful information about the rules for speech competitions (e.g. some speech tournament rules require the students to provide an ISBN or ISSN number for their sources). Students are also rewarded for originality, so coaches often suggest topics they feel students should consider (or topics to avoid because they have been used so frequently in tournaments). This information can be used to plan for the instruction sessions.

In June, the librarian contacts the Director of Summer Academic Programs to find out how registration for the camp is progressing and gets an estimate for the number of campers likely to attend. This is also an opportunity to share any library-related information with the Director (for example, changes to library hours or an interruption in Interlibrary Loan service during the week of the camp).

Several library staff members are involved in the planning process. For example, the Acquisitions Coordinator orders material for the camp, the Collection Manager (and her students) assists in pulling books from the stacks, and the Administrative Assistant handles the computer lab and room reservations.

After all of the early preparation, before the campers arrive the librarian will:
- Create online guide and handout
- Gather several reference works to use as examples
- Gather books related to each event category

COOKING METHOD

A blend of demonstration and hands-on exploration. Note: Session content varies slightly depending on whether students are preparing for informative events or interpretive events.

Introduction: welcome, distribute handouts, show students how to find the online guide, and a very brief overview of LC classification (5 min.)

FIGURE 1. Speech and Debate Camper handout

SELECTING A TOPIC
- Browse through issues of CQ Researcher - shelved in Reference at H35 .E352
- Look at the latest headlines on CNN.com or other news-related sites
- Browse through recent issues of magazines like the *Chronicle of Higher Education*, *Economist*, *Scientific American*, or *Atlantic Monthly*.
- Identify current events related to specific issues:
    o Legal issues – http://www.earlham.edu/~peters/courses/cle/clelinks.htm
    o Human services - http://www.handsnet.org
    o Government - http://www.usa.gov/Topics/Reference_Shelf/News.shtml
    o Environmental issues - http://www.envirolink.org
    o Science - http://www.nasonline.org

BACKGROUND INFORMATION
- CQ Researcher (Ref H 35 .E352) provides a wealth of background information
- Try a specialized encyclopedia – for example:
    o Oxford Encyclopedia of the Islamic World – Ref DS 35.53 .O96 2009
    o Gale Encyclopedia of Alternative Medicine – Ref R 733 .G34 2009
    o Encyclopedia of Environmental Ethics and Philosophy – Ref GE 42 .E533 2009
    o Encyclopedia of Organic, Sustainable, and Local Food – Ref HD 9005 .E645 2010
- Use MnPALS Plus to search for books. **Tip:** start by entering a broad term for the topic you're interested in.

For more detail, try...
- newspaper articles – use the following databases:
    o Lexis Nexis
    o ProQuest Newstand
- magazine and journal articles – start with a general database like:
    o Academic Search Premier
- **Tip:** Use connectors (AND, OR, NOT) and try putting phrases inside quotation marks.

- In pairs, students browse reference works (e.g. Granger's Index to Poetry or CQ Researcher) and are asked to share what they discover about the scope and organization of the reference work. The librarian and students discuss how reference works provide background information and may help students define or narrow their topic. (10 min.)

- In pairs, students search for a topic in the catalog. [During this time, students focused on interpretive events browse the tables and select a book from the examples provided.] Once they've found a book, they bring it back to the computer lab. Looking at the subject headings for the book, they conduct another search using one of the subject headings (e.g. "natural food industry" or "humorous fiction") and compare the results of this search to their first set of results. (15 min.)

- Students review the list of databases on the online guide and, based on the descriptions, select a database that fits their topic. The librarian offers a brief demonstration of search strategies and then students apply those strategies to their own topic. [During this time, students focused on interpretive events use an interdisciplinary database to search for poems and short stories published in literary journals.] (10 min.)

- Individually, students assess the results of their searches, noting the most successful keywords, fruitful call-number ranges, and relevant databases. (5 min.)

- Wrap-up. The librarian and students review the material covered in the session. Students are reminded of where and when the librarians are available at the reference desk. (5 min.)

Note: Reference assistance is provided during the week of the camp. Just as we would not expect college students to remember everything covered during a session, we view the instruction session as an introduction and encourage the campers to ask questions and discuss their topics with librarians.

ALLERGY WARNINGS

Although these students are similar to first-year students in some respects (e.g. unfamiliar with the specific library), it is important to remember that they are-younger and less experienced than first year college students. The students are typically bright and highly motivated, but their research backgrounds vary and some may need basic information on library services and collections. Furthermore, the camp environment and limited time frame create a fun and creative atmosphere but also foster stress and peer pressure. Therefore, while humor is always welcome in library instruction, it is especially appropriate during sessions like this one.

CHEF'S NOTE

Just as faculty participation is crucial in sessions with undergraduates, I have found it important to partner with the debate camp staff members and coaches. In addition to involving them in the instruction session, I also ask them questions about what they feel their students need to know or if there have been any changes in speech competition rules. The information they provide helps me to know where I need to tweak

the content or pedagogical approach during the sessions. Furthermore, the stronger the relationship with the debate coaches, the more likely they are to refer students to the reference desk during the camp.

ADDITIONAL RESOURCES

- Collins, Bobbie L. "Integrating Information Literacy Skills into Academic Summer Programs for Precollege Students." *Reference Services Review*, 37, no. 2 (2009): 143–154.
- Twait, Michelle L. Summer Speech Institute LibGuide. Folke Bernadotte Memorial Library. Last modified June 24, 2013. http://libguides.gustavus.edu/SSI.

Too Many Cooks in the Kitchen?
Improving Students' Research Approach by Providing Them with the Necessary Tools

Kimberly Davies-Hoffman, Coordinator of Instruction & Reference Services, Milne Library, SUNY Geneseo, kdhoffman@geneseo.edu; Dr. Paul Pacheco, Department of Anthropology, SUNY Geneseo, pacheco@geneseo.edu

NUTRITION INFORMATION

College level, any course where the goal is to have students dig deep into a specific topic that relates to the overall subject matter of the course

In order to have students fully understand the expectations of a comprehensive literature review assignment—subsequently teaching them the rigors, process and content of scholarly communication—it is essential that they see examples and models of what to include and what not to include in an annotated bibliography. It is also helpful that students engage in the process of determining the criteria upon which their annotated bibliographies would be assessed. Through both means (seeing examples of past work and determining assessment criteria), students enter into the project with a clear idea of what makes up an outstanding literature review and more importantly (to them), what will give them the highest grade.

Students
- Evaluate prior (unnamed) annotated bibliographies ranging from lower (draft version) grades to the highest in order to recognize best practices .

- Practice and perfect: accurate citation writing, searching comprehensively to identify the main scholars in the field, choosing to include scholarly over popular texts, justifying the selection of a popular article if appropriate to the overall body of research, making connections between scholars' work, locating more resources based on bibliographies and cited by references.
- Develop an assessment rubric (upon which their work would be based) in order to prepare themselves for the expectations of the annotated bibliography assignment.
- Use Google Docs to document the rubric and additional notes (simultaneously in-class) in order to refer back to the expectations as annotated bibliographies were completed.

Instructors
- Become consistent and systematic in their joint grading of the draft and final versions of each small group's annotated bibliography.
- Collaborate and reaffirm key names, topics and texts related to a small group's given subject

- Learn from each other about new approaches and tools for research topics in the field.

SERVES
No more than 30 students and they should be divided into small working groups. Ten group bibliographies to assess, staggered throughout the semester, is manageable

COOKING TIME
Class session: 50–75 minutes
Full project with grading/commenting on draft and final bibliography versions:1 semester

INGREDIENTS AND EQUIPMENT
- One professor willing to collaborate with an instruction librarian
- One librarian willing to teach at least one research session
- The same librarian who is willing to provide detailed feedback on each annotated bibliography and negotiate grades with the collaborating professor
- A computer classroom and/or student laptops
- Proficiency in using Google Docs in the classroom

- Examples of past student bibliographies to demonstrate varying levels of quality/scholarly comprehensiveness

PREPARATION

1. The professor clearly defines his/her objectives for a one-time research session. Should it be based on search skills, variety of library databases appropriate to the given topics, citation writing, or quality issues when researching and writing annotations?
2. The librarian gathers examples of low, mid and high level output of prior bibliography assignments.
3. The librarian coordinates groups within the library classroom (based on classroom layout and potential groupings) to work on various aspects of the class rubrics.
4. The librarian sets up the framework in Google Docs for a series of rubrics to be completed by students.
5. The librarian identifies potential databases and search strategies that could be useful to highlight during the course of the research session.

COOKING METHOD
Some background to this developing method

Students of an anthropology course are assigned (in small groups) a broad and reasonably well-known topic germane to North American archaeology and asked to comb the professional literature to develop a comprehensive annotated bibliography to accompany a 20-minute illustrated in-class presentation. There is a draft and final version of the bibliography which allows the students to learn from the gaps in information they may be missing from version 1 to 2. Through the process of librarian feedback, corrections and suggestions, along with collaborative grading between librarian and professor, students learn the art of scholarly research without expending too much of the professor's class time beyond a 50-minute lesson early in the semester.

The first time the librarian offered a scholarly research session (two sessions in Fall 2010), she focused on skills to lead students to the appropriate databases and employ useful search strategies. The second time, she was specifically asked to skip the lesson on searching and focus more heavily on what it takes to create a comprehensive annotated bibliography. In the professor's (paraphrased) words, "students can find the material, but you can help them make sure they understand the concept of a comprehensive annotated bibliography."

Spring 2012's scholarly research lesson consisted of the following activities:
In-class, library session
» Student evaluation of prior (unnamed) annotated bibliographies ranging from lower (draft version) grades to the highest
» Students developed a list of best practices of what to include, what to avoid and how to organize and connect within the bibliographic entries

» Student development of an assessment rubric upon which their draft and final grades for the annotated bibliography would be based
» Student use of Google Docs to document notes simultaneously (in-class) that they could refer back to as their annotated bibliographies were due

After library session
» The librarian looked at each draft annotated bibliography on their scheduled due dates, adding corrections to citation format, searching broadly for the given topic to help identify missing gaps in key resources/authors, skimming bibliographies of the sources included in the students' work to identify key resources/authors, reading annotations to verify (where appropriate) that connections were made from one scholar's work to another, suggesting additional databases and search methods to employ to complete the final version of the bibliography.
» The librarian would consult the student-developed rubric, highlighting the blocks of the rubric where students' work fell and suggested a grade to the collaborating professor.
» Professor and librarian agreed on a grade with additional notes of suggestion for the student group and the librarian forwarded the comments, grade and attached the highlighted rubric along with marked-up version (with librarian feedback) of the bibliography.

» The student-developed rubric assisted librarian and professor in being consistent and systematic in their joint grading of the draft and final versions of each small group's annotated bibliography.

» Student groups considered the librarian feedback, made the appropriate changes and turned in their final version (along with a formal presentation to the class).

ALLERGY WARNING

We have found that student groups receiving a high grade on their draft version of the bibliography may be inclined to ignore the librarian's suggestions and feedback and simply turn in the draft version as their final version, whereby doubling that high grade (where draft version grade is added to final version grade).

Detailed feedback and grading on the annotated bibliographies is time-consuming but gratifying work. Schedule your time accordingly and find ways to "work smart" (e.g., group students into manageable sizes so the collaborating faculty aren't looking through more than 10 bibliographies per semester, space the submission dates for each small group evenly throughout the semester, don't require students to submit 20+ resources for the bibliography).

Resist the temptation to fix all the students' mistakes. Remember that a librarian's feedback is meant to guide the students' work to a more improved and higher quality

state. In order to become lifelong learners, students need to see where corrections and resource additions need to be made along with simple explanations. They need to go through the process of making the corrections and/or seeking additional information. If a mistake is being made repeatedly, add "see" references to save yourself some time.

CHEFS' NOTE

As a second run of this collaborative annotated bibliography assignment, we have seen much improvement in the students' quality of scholarly work. With this more recent iteration, overall group grades have clustered in the high-mid to high level range of the possible 50 points (for each bibliography version—draft and final). In the first trial, before assigning the student-directed rubric activity, grades were widely scattered from low-mid to high level range. Consensus on assigning grades between the librarian and professor

has become much smoother with the rubric implementation and students are meeting the expectations that they developed within that Google Doc rubric.

With respect to our first cautionary tale above, in our third iteration of this collaborative project, we plan to require students to make the necessary changes from draft to final version if they are to receive a higher final grade. Another possible addition is to strongly encourage students to arrange for a one-on-one research consultation so many of the gaps needing to be filled can be discussed in person before the draft version of the bibliography is due.

One last possible adjustment, tackling cautionary tale #2, is to develop a method of bibliography peer-review so that students are learning the essential components of a comprehensive literature review in a multitude of ways:

FIGURE 1. Statistics illustrating students' improvement in work	
Fall 2010—draft grades, out of 50 points	**Spring 2012—draft grades, out of 50 points**
35–39 = 3 student bibliographies 40–43 = 1 student bibliography 44–47 = 6 student bibliographies 48–50 = 0 student bibliographies	35–39 = 0 student bibliographies 40–43 = 7 student bibliographies 44–47 = 6 student bibliographies 48–50 = 2 student bibliographies
Fall 2010—final grades, out of 50 points	**Spring 2012—final grades, out of 50 points**
35–39 = 0 student bibliographies 40–43 = 2 student bibliographies 44–47 = 6 student bibliographies 48–50 = 2 student bibliographies 51+ = 1 student bibliography (52)	35–39 = 1 student bibliography 40–43 = 2 student bibliographies 44–47 = 5 student bibliographies 48–50 = 7 student bibliographies

- Through examples of varying quality during the scheduled research session
- Through the collaborative development of a grading rubric (in class and later posted on the course site)
- Through the review of a preceding group's annotated bibliography
- Through meeting with a librarian one-on-one
- Through completion of their own annotated bibliography—once as a draft, followed by librarian feedback to help them perfect the final version.

ADDITIONAL RESOURCES

- The Google Doc rubric developed by Spring 2012 ANTH 207 students: http://bit.ly/yC4WvL

Twitter Tapas for Embedded Librarianship:
"Byte-size" Course Integrated Literacy Instruction While Engaging Students in Almost-Synchronous Virtual Reference

Carol Hartmann Adjunct Online Instructor—Library Technical Assistant Program, Waubonsee Community College, chartmann@waubonsee.edu, Twitter accounts: @ltaparaprof, @ltaconnect, and @libraryportals

Byte #1: Tapas originated in southern Spain but tapas bars have now opened all over the world.[1]

NUTRITION INFORMATION

Twitter "Tapas" are curated by embedded librarians in "byte-size" servings as an effective method to collect existing knowledge, links, media files; to construct professional learning communities; to develop discipline-based information literacy; and to inspire lifelong learners and mentors to share their knowledge base.

The distance learning, teacher-librarian embedded in a course management system can recommend course related documents, links, and multimedia at the point of information need using dynamic Twitter presentation tools such as re-tweets, favorites, #hashtags, lists, and linked newsletters. The embedded librarian performs a liaison role in collaboration with course instructors and program directors using subject areas of expertise to map information literacy goals to student learning outcomes. Staff collaboration creates opportunities to deliver cross-discipline content, to continue conversations with students after course completion, and to research significant Twitter threads.

Byte #2: Tapas are served in cafeteria-style displays; or a server may recite a list of what is available well-versed like a poem; or a detailed menu is presented for customers to find familiar favorites or sample new dishes.[2]

INGREDIENTS AND EQUIPMENT

- Twitter account
- Laptop or mobile device
- Other social media content links can include but are not limited to: Scoop.it (content curation), Google+ (hangout/screencast), Slideshare (presentation), Pinterest (virtual bulletin board), YouTube Channels (videos).

The embedded librarian performs a liaison role with teaching staff responsible for media creation and curates links to webscale multimedia content.

Byte #3: Tapas are easy to prepare at home, and it is common to serve a small homemade tapas to nibble before sitting down to the main meal.[3]

PREPARATION

To read tweets posted by others, participants must create accounts profiles, which are linked with e-mail accounts that are used to send updates for account verification. Users can then post their own micro-blogs that contain small pieces of digital content such as text, pictures, links, short videos, or other media on the Internet. Groups of professional colleagues, embedded librarians, and online students frequently update content and follow each other's post in the collaborative process of creating a learning community to support curriculum standards (K–12), course syllabi in degree programs (higher education), or professional development (continuing education). Whatever the instructional level, information literacy is embedded in student learning outcomes, expressed 140 characters at a time. The embedded librarian is trained in subject analysis and authority work to evaluate microblog content.

COOKING METHOD

Online Pedagogy is Problem Based Learning (PBL) that facilitates active engagement with course content to meet Student Learning Objectives (SLOs).

Byte #4 Tapas can be served hot or cold.[4]

Hot Tapas Plate 1 requires active participation and account management by Twitter participants. PBL SLO #1 is to create a profile that clearly identifies the professional, instructional, or research purpose for all Twitter posts. This purpose challenges all participants to focus on defining how social media goals using Twitter successfully meet student learning objectives. The embedded librarian role is to integrate information literacy instruction into significant course related activities.

Byte #5 Tapas can be small portions of any of the dishes that make up Spain's wide and varied cuisine.[5]

Hot Tapas Plate 2 considers every tweet to be an act of transparent, transliterate, transformative leadership in making public posts. PBL SLO #2 is to consider the limitation of 140 characters to convey meaning and requires skill with technical writing for the web as well as technical knowledge of how to link digital formats.

URLs can be shortened with various utilities. Document links can be shared by uploading content to Google drives and granting public permissions to view. Using tweets to share content in a wide variety of formats can be a virtual lesson in digital literacy for instructors, students, and mentors who are more or less tech-savvy about file formats and webscale collaboration. The # symbol,

called a hashtag, is used to mark keywords or topics in a tweet. It was created organically by Twitter users as a way to categorize messages. The embedded librarian can generate value-added content with subject-based #hashtags to increase intellectual access. Librarians can curate content using social media newsletters such as Scoop.it. Instructional Multimedia Content can be dynamically linked using other social media tools such as Google+, Pinterest, Slideshare or YouTube.

Byte #6 A social ritual has developed for gathering to have tapas, giving people an opportunity for conversation with others.[6]

Hot Tapas Plate 3 ensures that participants actively practice digital citizenship and follow rules for netiquette when creating tweets. PBL SLO #3 simulates in-class discussions and presentations translated to tweets. Students online must follow the same protocol as face-to-face interactions but require participants to understand the differences in-group dynamics when conversations are limited to 140 characters. Introducing the Student Peer Review process encourages transparent "thinking out loud" with public posts that facilitate student collaboration and communication about their own information search process. Embedded librarians can introduce essential information literacy topics at critical points such as how to refine a focus topic, how to improve search results, how to evaluate web sources and how to cite sources properly. Librar-

ians can model good netiquette as outlined in best practices for text-based reference interviews. Improving social media skills can increase competitive advantage with guided practice and feedback from embedded librarians.

Byte #7 eaten with fingers informally, or served formally with a fork and a small piece of bread.[7]

Cold Tapas Plate 1 typically serves a "small piece of bread" on which different toppings are placed. The single most important task to address before using Twitter to develop a professional learning community is to draft or review your social media policy for library user instruction at your learning institution. This requirement involves direct conversations with marketing and public relations, program directors, distance learning support, and library faculty liaisons. Having a mission statement and mapping instructional goals and objectives to academic courses and programs can help to define the list of what is available, helping embedded librarians explain to institutional stakeholders why Twitter is a useful tool for specific instructional purposes. Institutional branding, grade-appropriate intended audiences, and ALA ethics statements are other considerations for evaluating social media policies. Twitter feeds that are carefully constructed and moderated by embedded librarians create teachable moments about digital citizenship for responsible administrators, faculty, staff, and students.

Byte #8 Often people do not stay in just one place, but move from tapas bar to tapas bar enjoying the specialties served in each one.[8]

Cold Tapas Plate 2 involves low-stakes methods to get started. One low-stakes starter to gain experience generating a professional mix of Twitter streams is to follow innovative stakeholders such as embedded librarians, distance librarians, or instructional librarians who actively curate credible lists of Twitter followers, following, and favorites. Re-tweets are an easy way to acknowledge credible content worth sharing with colleagues or students. Subject specialties in Twitter conversations are identified with #hashtags to facilitate ongoing conversations about K–12 core curriculums, academic programs, and research activities. Another easy method for learning how to microblog is for attendees to tweet about presenters at professional development events, online webinars, conferences, and meetings. Twitter educators, academics, and researchers typically limit shared content to professional resources.

Byte #9 A social ritual has developed for gathering to have tapas, giving people an opportunity for conversation with others.[9]

Cold Tapas Plate 3 has ingredients for improving Twitter conversations to make connections. Setting up a Twitter account including profile and preferences involves branding Twitter participants so that like-minded learners can connect. Precision in key terms and phrases is essential so that the best contacts (mentors/subject experts) can find and connect with the professional learning community. Getting started with branding requires a significant commitment to care and feeding of followers on a regular basis. Daily review at the start of each day to research who is followed and who follows your account can ensure a public profile linked to credible resources. Another strategy is to check who a follower is following to determine whether their purpose is primarily professional and to identify other subject experts they are already following. Librarians who use Twitter often create organized lists to increase relevance by collecting and connecting groups of Twitter users focused on select topics.

Byte #10 On special occasions, this ritual can take place over a longer period with participants taking turns buying a round of dishes for their social group.[10]

Large Tapas Plates for sharing with a crowd, served by embedded librarians, can model effective techniques for both how to start and how to sustain professional learning communities. Putting this Twitter Tapas menu together is intended to help embedded librarians get started to discover familiar favorites or sample new dishes.

10 Tips for getting started using Twitter for instruction and professional development:

1. Learn Twitter lingo from the Twitter help center while setting up your Twitter account.
2. Read tweet streams on timelines to facilitate reflection and formative assessment using best practices for evaluating webscale information.
3. Find interesting accounts that introduce a discovery platform across a wide range of disciplines to broaden coverage. See who those who you follow are following to increase relevance and to narrow coverage.
4. Click links embedded in others tweets to view documents, images, videos, podcasts, webinar recordings, and websites to include content from a wide range of formats.
5. Click hashtags# to view all tweets about topics and see who has contributed to the conversation using principles of authority work.
6. Build a voice to establish your area of subject expertise by mentioning others and retweeting their essential microblogs.
7. Subscribe to lists created by others and view a list timeline to show a stream of tweets from only the users on that list.
8. Connect your mobile accounts with Twitter accounts to follow trending topics.
9. Connect your social media content from dynamic 2.0 tools you curate: Google+ or Pinterest.
10. Follow embedded librarian accounts that add value in transparent peer review, transliterate collaboration, and transformative mentoring. Embed your own librarian to actively construct and continue this conversation.

TABLE 1. Recommended Twitter accounts

Top 10 Embedded Librarians to follow	Top 10 Distance Librarian #Hashtags	Top 10 Twitter Tribes	Top 10 Librarian Social Media
@davidshumaker	#tlchat	@rmbyrne	@twitter
@rashford	#elearning	@BestofDL	@diigo
@IDLibrarian	#edtech	@ACRL_DLS	@Pinterest
@dmcordell	#lrnchat	@digpublib	@YouTube
@jenniferlagarde	#disted	@teachthought	@MentorMob
@heyjudeonline	#openbadges	@twittbraries	@scoopit
@libraryfuture	#DLchat	@edutopia	@slideshare
@joycevalenza	#curation	@projectSAILS	@springshare
@buffyjhamilton	#library	@librarycongress	@wordpress
@gwenythjones	#libfuture	@C4LPT	@mlearningschool

ADDITIONAL RESOURCES
- Google URL shortener http://goo.gl/
- Google Drive https://drive.google.com/
- Scoop.it http://www.scoop.it/

NOTES
1. Ortega, Simone and Inés Ortega. 2010. *The Book of Tapas*. New York: Phaidon.
2. Ibid.
3. Ibid.
4. Ibid.
5. Ibid.
6. Ibid.
7. Ibid.
8. Ibid.
9. Ibid.
10. Ibid.

2. First Courses: Embedding in the First Year Experience

Many librarians experience success embedding in the first year experience (FYE) at colleges and universities. There is something special about being a part of the learning community that occurs when students are new to college life. The first year experience provides many opportunities for librarians to engage meaningfully with students, and sets the stage for a good relationship for the rest of their careers.

Most librarians who teach traditional one-shot library instruction sections know at least one instructor who says, "We love our library visit so much, I wish we could come one or two more times at least!" If this sounds familiar, you have just identified the perfect partner for an embedded instruction project and a willing collaborator for the ideas presented in this section.

Steps to Success:
Exploring the Research Process with First-Year Students

Andrea Falcone, University of Northern Colorado, andrea.falcone@unco.edu

SETTING
Technology-equipped classroom where students can work in small groups

NUTRITION INFORMATION
Designed specifically for first-year students, this session asks groups to become familiar with the research process using hands-on tasks and critical thinking. Students develop a research strategy on a given topic, find/access resources (books and peer-reviewed journal articles), explore services (Interlibrary Loan), and evaluate resources. Two quick assessments are embedded within the activity for easy data collection. The research process is broken into logical steps, and the sample topic can be tailored to any discipline or subject area.

SERVES
Classes of approximately 25 students are recommended as students work in groups of three or four to ensure participation from each member.

COOKING TIME
This 50-minute library session is embedded into each First-Year Experience course taught every fall.

INGREDIENTS AND EQUIPMENT
- Computers with Internet access for student groups
- Individually printed worksheets (one sheet for each of the six steps)
- The first page of a peer-reviewed journal article, including the abstract
- The first page of a popular article, including the abstract
- The first page of a bibliography/references list from the peer-reviewed journal article above
- Assessment checklist

PREPARATION
- Print copies of worksheets for groups
- Print an assessment checklist
- Check-out book mentioned in Step 2 if students are to explore Interlibrary Loan options

COOKING METHOD
Break students into groups of three or four and expose them to the research process asking them to complete six steps/worksheets. Once groups finish a step, they notify the librarian, and he/she will comment verbally on the worksheet and hand out the next step. Depending on the target learning outcome(s), librarians can conduct a quick assessment when checking on groups

prior to moving them to the next step. For example, one learning outcome may include determining if students could identify appropriate keywords and create a search string.

Step 1 asks students to accomplish this task. As the librarian checks to see if groups are ready to move to Step 2, he/she can use the Assessment Checklist to mark whether a group is successful.

FIGURE 1. Sample Assessment Checklist

Instructor:

Date:

When students complete Step 1, note if groups are successful and mark columns below with a checkmark. If groups are unsuccessful, mark columns with an "x."

Learning Outcome: Identify appropriate keywords and search strings		
	(a.) Students can generate lists of synonyms for a given topic.	(b.) Students can generate search strings without prepositions.
Group/Row 1		
Group/Row 2		
TOTAL:	✓	✓
	✗	✗

Additionally, the final worksheet asks students to determine two important concepts learned during the session. Doing so serves two purposes: (1) it provides useful and interesting data for the librarians, and (2) it engages groups in a useful, but nonessential task if they finished well before the rest of the class.

Step 1: Developing your topic and search string

Topic: I am interested in researching the connections between child obesity and fast food.

List keywords for the topic below. Then list one synonym for each keyword.

keyword	keyword	keyword
synonym	synonym	synonym

A *search string* includes keywords usually combined with the word **AND**. You can try multiple search strings when looking for resources to get different results. Create a search string using the terms above:

_____

Step 2: Finding resources—books

Use your search string to find a **book** and fill in the following:

Book title:

Author(s):

Location:

Call Number:

Is the book available?

Can you borrow a copy of the book *Remembering Heart Mountain: Essays on Japanese American Internment in Wyoming* edited by Mike Mackey from the Michener Library? If not, describe how you would get a copy from somewhere else. (Hint: Look for Prospector.)

Step 3: Locating books (and other materials) on the shelves

There are over a million volumes in the Michener Library, and most volumes are arranged by the Library of Congress (LC) Call Number System. Put these call numbers in the order they would appear on the shelf. (Hint: Call numbers are arranged in alphabetical and then numerical order.)

____ RJ449 R88 1975

____ PC4261.R5 1992

____ PE1617.094 W558 2003

____ PC4121.H37 1998

Locations:
Call numbers A–F are on the 2nd floor
Call numbers G–Z are on the 3rd floor

These call numbers would be found on which floor of the Michener Library?

Step 4: Finding more resources—journal articles

Use your search string to find a **journal article** that is peer reviewed and fill in the following:

Journal Article Title:

Journal Title:

Author(s):

Month (if available) and Year of Publication:

Volume/Issue/Page Numbers:

Can you find a copy of the following article through the UNC Libraries? If not, describe how you would get a copy from somewhere else.

"Child body mass index, obesity, and proximity to fast food restaurants" written by J. M. Mellor in 2011

Step 5: Evaluating resources

When you find resources, you'll want to evaluate them to determine if they are related to your topic. Attached are abstracts for two peer-reviewed journal articles. An *abstract* is a summary of the article. Skim the attached abstracts and determine if the articles seem relevant to your topic. If the abstract is relevant, highlight important words/phrases/ideas that helped you determine its relevancy. If the abstract is not relevant, explain why under the abstract.

Part 6: Finding additional sources

Many of the resources you find will include references—in other words, research from other sources. If the references seem useful and relevant to your topic, you can track them down. Let's try that now! Use the attached references list to find one additional resource. Show the instructor that you have found a copy.

The final step for students is the Wrap-Up: As a group, determine two important things you learned during the session and write them down.

ALLERGY WARNINGS

Librarians that feel most comfortable conducting a catalog or database demonstration may need to practice this technique as maintaining awareness of group progress can be challenging. Some groups may benefit from a little guidance, but be careful not to reveal answers before allowing students to explore choices and think critically.

CHEF'S NOTE

In the past, engaging students in first-year courses devoid of corresponding research assignments was a challenge. This fast-paced, 50-minute session is filled with teaching moments and groups buzzing with activity. The minimal preparation, student exposure to the research process, and easily-collected assessments are worth a try!

Avoiding Plagiarism—Don't Get Burned

Cate Calhoun Ovaret, Auburn University, ccalhoun@auburn.edu

NUTRITION INFORMATION

This recipe gives students a taste of plagiarism: what it is and how to avoid sneaky surprises. It also allows a librarian embedded in a First-Year Experience program a chance to make a connection with students so they may begin to build their relationship with the library.

Many first-year students come to college having only done "research" in the sense of regurgitating the ideas of others in summary format. This module of library instruction for First Year Experience students introduces freshman to the subtle forms of plagiarism so they can identify and avoid them. It is also the first step in encouraging students to think for themselves and use research to support their own ideas.

COOKING TIME

50 Minutes

INGREDIENTS AND EQUIPMENT

- Interactive quiz
- Group worksheet
- Individual mini paper
- Instructor's computer with projection
- iClickers
- Identification worksheets
- Mini-paper prompts

PREPARATION

- Set up interactive quiz and iClickers
- Copies of handouts

COOKING METHOD

1. Students share their thoughts on what is considered plagiarism. They are introduced to the five types of plagiarism: Cut and Paste, Word Switch Style, Metaphor and Idea.
2. Students work in small groups to compare writing samples to the original source material. They identify whether or not plagiarism has occurred and what type it is.
3. The entire class discusses each example looking at what went wrong and how it could have been improved.
4. Students individually complete "mini-papers." They summarize a short article about a current event in two to three sentences, using the techniques they have learned to avoid plagiarizing the material.

ALLERGY WARNING

Encourage discussion while the worksheet is being completed. The answers are not obvious. Students need to know that it's less important to name the type of the plagiarism than it is to know to avoid it!

CHEF'S NOTE

This material can be a little dry—spice things up with an article for the mini paper about an event in popular culture. Something the students have been talking about already or breaking news from that day works well to bring up the energy towards the end of the class period. Don't forget to remind students that the reference desk is a great place to visit for citation help!

Eat Dessert First!
Flipping the Sequence of Information Literacy Instruction to Enhance Student Learning

Nancy Fawley, Head of Library Liaison Program, University of Nevada Las Vegas, nancy.fawley@unlv.edu

NUTRITION INFORMATION

The basic technique used here is the flipped classroom where lecture-type content is assigned before class and in-class time is spent reviewing and applying the concepts. There are many opportunities during class time to incorporate active-learning techniques such as group work, discussions and hands-on activities. This recipe can be adapted to work with any subject area or discipline.

SERVES

This approach to instruction works best with class sizes of less than 30, but it can be adapted to larger groups.

COOKING TIME

The length of this project is flexible. A flipped classroom approach can be used for every class or selected classes where the concepts would best be learned by in-class, hands-on activities.

INGREDIENTS AND EQUIPMENT

- Podcasts or videos related to learning outcomes. These can be homemade or prepared by a vendor or other "chef"
- Activity or assignment related to the learning objects that is completed prior to class
- Optional: In-class assignment or quiz that serves to assess student learning

COOKING METHOD

The Flipped Classroom

PREPARATION

Learning objects and assignments must be prepared in advance. Creating tutorials can be time consuming; however, once the initial preparation of developing learning objects and assignments is completed, they can be reused indefinitely as long as the content is current and they continue to meet the learning objectives of the class. Developing the content for a three-to-five minute video or podcast can take a few hours to a few days depending on your command of the content and the technology you will be using. You can shorten the preparation time by using existing tutorials, such as vender-produced videos on specific databases or resources and use these on their own or in combination with self-produced content. To be effective, however, in-class and out-of-class activities must be integrated and address stated learning outcomes.

Another important part of the preparation is meeting with the faculty or instructor you will be working with during your library instruction. It is important to explain the concept of the flipped classroom and your intended lesson plans and learning outcomes, both pre-class and during class. The success of this instruction can hinge on the support you get from the instructor, especially related to the pre-class homework and assignment. Students are more likely to complete the work before class if instructors require it for a day grade or other type of credit. Completion of the pre-class tasks is essential for the flipped classroom approach to library instruction to be effective.

THE EMBEDDED PROJECT

A flipped classroom is a pedagogical model that reverses lecture and homework. Instead of a lecture in class and hands-on work at home, instructors assign material to be reviewed ahead of time, allowing for problem-solving activities during class time. Librarians can apply a similar approach to their embedded library instruction. Students listen to podcasts or view videos related to lecture content prior to attending class. This frees up class time and allows the librarian and students to focus on reviewing and applying what was learned. Allowing students to do hands-on work in class brings an active-learning element and opportunity for critical thinking that is often lacking in traditional library instruction. And, it gives librarians a chance to work more closely with students while they are engaged in their research. The combination of synchronous and asynchronous learning opportunities can also better address different types of learners.

This specific recipe was developed for two classes embedded into a freshman composition class. The first class focuses on keyword development, while the second class focuses on evaluating the reliability and relevance of different types of sources. Both classes have short, Jeopardy-style quizzes to accompany the podcasts. If time allows, reviewing the assignment in class will help you to gauge which concepts the students are struggling with. The podcasts and quizzes were created with the intent that students should not need to spend more than 30 to 45 minutes to complete the assignment.

For the first class, students listened to podcasts on developing search terms, boolean operators, and creating search strings and basic searching using a discovery tool. A short *Jeopardy*-style assignment was developed to test the students' comprehension of the content; students write a question to the given answer. In class, students worked on a worksheet to develop keyword search terms based on their own research topics.

They then were able to use these terms to search for resources using the library's discovery tool. The librarian was able to work with each student on their search terms and strategy, while the instructor was available to assist their students on topic and assignment-related issues.

For the second class, podcasts were assigned on the difference between an article and a book, scholarly and popular sources, and the reliability of Google to search for sources. Another *Jeopardy*-style quiz was assigned. In class, students worked on an evaluation worksheet where they found a source related to their research topic and evaluated it for reliability and relevance.

ALLERGY WARNINGS

Teaching in a flipped classroom manner requires advanced preparation. Tutorials or podcasts must be created that address the concepts that will be covered in class. Having an assignment that students complete to test their understanding of the tutorial content helps students retain the information and gives the librarian an opportunity to assess student learning.

CHEF'S NOTE

The unscripted nature of the in-class session may be challenging, especially at first as unexpected questions and problems may arise. Librarians may be expected to answer questions or assist with research problems that they have not prepared for. Students, unfamiliar with this style of instruction, may

also resist the participative interaction a flipped classroom requires of them. Skipping or taking shortcuts on the preparation can lead to an unsavory experience.

ADDITIONAL RESOURCES

- 7 things you should know about… flipped classrooms." (2012). *Educause Learning Initiative*. Retrieved from http://educause.edu/eli.
- Berrett, D. How 'flipping' the classroom can improve the traditional lecture. *Chronicle of Higher Education* 58.25 (2012). Retrieved from http://chronicle.com/article/How-Flipping-the-Classroom/130857.
- TED-Ed: Lessons worth sharing. (2012). TED Conferences LLC. Retrieved from http://ed.ted.com/videos. (*This is a resource that allows you to "flip" a video from YouTube and add a quiz or other supplementary materials.*)

Sauté, Simmer, Reduce:
Embedded Lessons in the Research Process for First-Year Composition Students

Robin E. Miller, Research & Instruction Librarian, University of Wisconsin-Eau Claire, millerob@uwec.edu

NUTRITION INFORMATION

This recipe supports students through the process of writing a research paper, from narrowing a topic, to searching for information, to revising the research. The embedded lessons described in this recipe foster a connection between students and librarians, maintaining strong supports between the classroom, the assignment, and the library while exposing students to the iterative process of research. Introducing students to topic selection strategies prior to the class session in which they search for information enables them to consider their interests and mull over potential approaches. When students bring their "mind-maps" to the second session, they enthusiastically blend their keywords into the search activities, and they are prepared to revise their search terms because the mind-map offers plentiful alternatives. The final embedded lesson helps students to continue to refine their research skills, showing them that research continues throughout the writing and revision process.

SERVES

This recipe is best for undergraduate courses in which students engage in rhetorical and inquiry-based writing exercises, including first-year composition courses with 20–30 students.

COOKING TIME

Four to six weeks

INGREDIENTS AND EQUIPMENT

- One energetic instruction librarian/chef
- One collaborating instructor/chef
- One research assignment
- Networked computer access for all students
- Instructor station
- Blackboard/whiteboard
- Web-based guide for just-in-time reminders and skill-building

PREPARATION

- Establish relationship with collaborating instructor.
- To coincide with appropriate due dates, schedule 3 embedded lessons by instruction librarian: One 20-minute discussion of paper topic ideas; one 50-minute instructional session; and one 50-minute follow-up instructional or work session.
- Between each embedded lesson, librarian and instructor must communicate to exchange information about student challenges and progress.

COOKING METHOD
Sauté (20 minutes)

To sauté, we heat a pan with a little fat and quickly fry the recipe's foundational ingredients, tossing and stirring from time to time until everything is softened and ready for the next step. In this recipe, we visit the classroom for introductions, discuss potential paper topics, and prepare for the next step.

1. Solicit a volunteer to write research topic on the board and using ideas offered by students in the class, guide the volunteer through drawing a "mind-map" or "concept map" on the board.

2. Ask students to create their own "mind-maps" by saying, "Now that you have watched us create a mind map, think about your own paper topic. Before our next class meeting, map out the ideas related to the topic and bring the map to our next class meeting. We're going to use your mind map when we search for information."

3. Optional: The librarian and course instructor may choose to make the concept map a point-based activity with grades assigned by the instructor, the librarian, or both. If you make that decision, inform the students that their mind map will be graded.

4. Show students how to locate the web-based research guide for the course.

Simmer (50 minutes)

To simmer, we add more ingredients to the sauté pan, reduce the heat to low, and allow all the flavors to mingle. In this recipe, we meet for a second time to incorporate previously-selected topics into instruction about searching for information.

FIGURE 1. Example student mind map of search terms

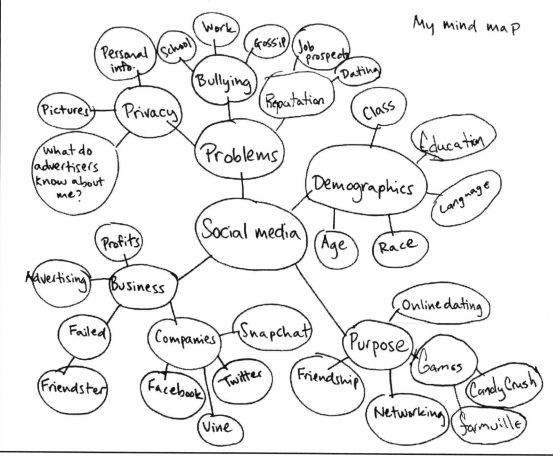

1. Welcome students to the computer lab. (1–2 minutes)
2. Ask students to share their mind-maps with you and with each other; encourage students to suggest additions to each other's mind-maps. (3–5 minutes)
3. Solicit a volunteer and use the concepts and keywords in his or her mind-map to demonstrate keyword searching in a database or discovery interface. (3–5 minutes)

4. Ask the students to find a partner. Ask each student to enter a database or discovery interface and use his or her partner's keywords and concepts to find a resource relevant to the partner's topic. Circulate through the class, troubleshooting, and noting successful strategies to highlight for the class. The partner search activity was developed by librarians and English composition faculty at the University of Wisconsin-Eau Claire.[1] (5–7 minutes)
5. Interrupt partner search. Ask students to share the challenges or roadblocks they experienced as they searched for information for their partner. Discuss and demonstrate possible remedies, including revision of search terms, narrowing search results, and use of facets and controlled vocabulary offered by databases. Show students how to send search results to their partners. (7–10 minutes)
6. Ask the students to enter a database or discovery interface and use the keywords from their own mind-map to search for a resource related their own research topic. Circulate among the class, troubleshooting, offering individual suggestions, and reminding students how to save or send themselves relevant information. (15–20 minutes)
7. Wrap-up. Remind students of the location of the class research guide. Encourage individual appointments. (2–3 minutes)

Reduce (50 minutes)

To reduce is to thicken and intensify the flavor of a sauce. In this recipe we meet for a third time after receiving a grade and comments on a draft of the research paper. We revisit the topics and skills previously developed, reevaluating sources, and refining the research.

1. Welcome the students back to the computer lab. (1–2 minutes)
2. Ask students about the sources they used and whether they found "enough" sources. Troubleshoot problems using tools to find sources. (5–10 minutes)
3. Ask students how they evaluated the sources they integrated into their papers. Solicit examples from reference lists in student papers and project one or two examples to the screen so that the entire class can view the sources. Ask a volunteer to describe what is known about the purpose, audience, and author of a source. Ask students to discuss the reasons that purpose, audience, or author influence the quality of information offered by a source. This exercise allows students to compare and contrast sources, using these factors to understand the context in which information is created. For example, students might observe that the purpose of a video posted by a news network immediately after a tragic event might be to inform the audience of breaking news, but information may be incomplete or incorrect. A tweet, blog post, or editorial may offer one individual's opinion or insights into the event. A newspaper article published days, weeks, or months after the event may offer a fuller set of facts and analysis of the event. A scholarly article may mention or discuss the event, or events like it, in the context of a larger trend, issue, or problem. (15–20 minutes)
4. Challenge the students to diversify or improve their sources using library databases and freely available websites, considering purpose, audience, and authorship as a strategy for evaluating sources. Circulate among the students and look at each student's reference list, offering individual consultation where necessary. (20 minutes)
5. Optional: Depending on the nature of the collaboration with the instructor, the librarian may play a role in grading the draft and resubmitted reference lists. In that case, the librarian should obtain copies of the draft and final papers.

FIGURE 2. Students work in pairs to search for information using their mind maps.

6. Wrap-up. Remind students of the location of the class research guide. Encourage individual appointments. (2–3 minutes)

ALLERGY WARNINGS

The full cooperation of a collaborating instructor is essential to this recipe's success. The author of this recipe is not involved in grading mind maps, reference lists, or other elements of student work. However, the librarian and classroom instructor communicate frequently between each embedded lesson about student progress, in order to ensure that the librarian can season the next embedded lesson with ingredients authentic to student development.

The author is embedded in one to two courses per semester. The three embedded lessons described in this recipe have not been scaled to the more than 50 one-shot instruction sessions delivered each semester by librarians at the University of Wisconsin-Eau Claire; however the partner search activity ("Simmer") is a consistent feature of one-shot instruction at the author's library. Instructors who cannot accommodate three embedded sessions can introduce the mind mapping activity ("Sauté") with a short video about concept mapping which students watch independently prior to a one-shot session with a librarian. While the follow-up session ("Reduce") helps students to refine their research and writing, some instructors may choose to engage students on the topic of source evaluation independently of a librarian.

CHEF'S NOTE

This instruction is assessed with a survey delivered to students and faculty at the conclusion of each semester. Anecdotal evidence indicates that students appreciate the opportunity to refine their search skills with a librarian over time. This embedded lesson offers new undergraduates the opportunity to develop a relationship with a librarian over the course of a semester. In addition, these embedded lessons facilitate a conversation between undergraduates who are engaged in a recursive, inquiry-based project, fostering low-stakes opportunities for students to converse and exchange ideas about topics and sources.

ADDITIONAL RESOURCES

- In addition to the three embedded class meetings, this recipe is enhanced with a web-based research guide (http://libguides.uwec.edu/topics) to assist students when they reach a roadblock while working independently.
- A partner search activity (Watson et al., 2013) is incorporated into all first-year composition instruction taught by librarians at UW-Eau Claire, regardless of whether a librarian is embedded with the course.

NOTE

1. Watson, S. E., Rex, C., Markgraf, J. Kishel, H., Jennings, E., Hinnant, K. (2013). "Revising the 'One-shot' through Lesson Study: Collaborating with Writing Faculty to Rebuild a Library Instruction Session." *College & Research Libraries,* 74(4), 381–398.

From Smorgasbord to Sous-Chef:
Communities of Practice in Information Literacy

Marianne Giltrud, Catholic University of America, giltrud@cua.edu

NUTRITION INFORMATION

The goal of this recipe is to teach students the research skills necessary to discover, evaluate and integrate knowledge grounded in reflection, metacognition, and analysis. The embedded librarian program incorporates teaching, learning and assessment to ensure students develop lifelong learning skills.

BACKGROUND

Catholic University Libraries has had a systematic program of library instruction since 2002. However, a more formal exploration of information literacy instruction and embedded librarianship emerged in a variety of contexts since its LibQual+ Satisfaction Survey 2008 and the 2008 Middle States Accreditation Self-Study. As a very organic process, the University embarked on its First Year Experience Program. Starting small and making changes each year, the program developed from its infancy into a mature program. Moreover, as the First Year Experience Program developed, so too did the University Libraries in response to the LibQual+ findings as well as its Information Literacy Instruction Program. It was not all easy going.

In the fall of 2009, with the Middle States Accreditation site visit planned for spring 2010, the University decided to launch a more formal First Year Experience Program. At the same time, the University embarked on its Strategic Plan Process that concluded in April 2012 with the Board of Trustees final approval. Taking a unique approach, the FYE program was organized around learning communities with the emphasis on liberal arts education. The foundational courses of theology, philosophy and writing, framed the context for the Learning Communities.

Similarly, the ENGLISH 101 curriculum was changed to a focus on rhetoric and logic from rhetoric and writing. It was during this iteration of the FYE program that information literacy instruction changed from a regularly scheduled part of the ENGLISH 101 curriculum for each section to an as requested basis. By mid semester it was clear that this was not working. What at first seemed insurmountable proved to be a blessing in disguise. The University Libraries faced disruption head on, managed change and proved it was a key player to the success of the university at large.

SERVES

18–20 students

COOKING TIME

Length of Project: 2008–2012

INGREDIENTS AND EQUIPMENT

- Learning Communities of Practice and first-year curriculum built around three foundational courses in philosophy, English and theology.
- Blackboard or other learning management system
- Digital classroom for library instruction
    » Lecture style classroom
    » 22 computer work stations
    » Instructor Podium with a PC or Laptop
        ◊ Projector
        ◊ Screen
- LibGuides for Writing Logic and Rhetoric (ENGLISH 101) and Faith Seeking Understanding (Theology and Religious Studies TRS 201)

PREPARATION

- Meet with faculty at the beginning of the semester to discuss goals.
    » Ask to be added as an instructor in Blackboard

» Review syllabus, research assignment and rubric
» Create library assignment and instruction module based on course rubric and information literacy learning outcomes.

- Participate in as many learning communities events i.e, orientation, social, and educational.
  » Orientation
  » FYE speaker series
  » D.C. Excursions
  » FYE dinners and breakfasts

- Be brave! Try new things. Be willing to fail forward. Most embedded librarianship programs are typically approached from a single focus having many definitions and iterations. This technique incorporates information literacy learning outcomes, library as a place, marketing, engagement, enthusiasm and a holistic approach to teaching and learning. Moreover, when balanced against a five year period of great change not only in academic libraries but in our unique library, i.e. new University President, Middle States Accreditation, Strategic Plan, Master Plan, staff changes, and budget cuts, I believe our recipe for change can serve as a model for others to learn how a small private institution with limited funds can move with the times. What this means is that you can do it by starting small and learning from your mistakes.

Expect push back and yes even reticence, but keep focused on the goal. Step by step, change occurs when not expected.

ALLERGY WARNING
- Don't give up. It's not always smooth sailing. Look for teachable moments and refine your teaching skills.
- Reflect on what worked best for each instruction session, interaction and make improvements.
- Use instruction examples tailored to what the student is learning.
- Timing is important.
- Be a team player. Get involved. Be a friendly face.
- Creativity, enthusiasm and smiles are encouraged.

CHEF'S NOTE
- Incorporate more on citations, citation managers and bibliographies.
- Provide more examples of narrowing the topic.
- Consider office hours from as needed to regularly schedule in a place where students meet.

INSTRUCTIONAL RESOURCES:
- Blackboard
- Digital Classroom
- LibGuides
- Electronic Databases, E-Books and print collections
- Social networking sites such as Facebook, Twitter, etc.
- The Library as a Place: comfy chairs,

FYE reading room, reading rooms, group study, individual and quiet study areas

COOKING METHOD
Game changing outreach and engagement
To explicitly articulate the return on investment derived from the University Libraries, specifically information literacy instruction, a proactive approach was mandated. What better way to show value than by creating learning outcomes? Therefore, an assertive program of outreach, engagement and collaboration ensued.

The result was a specific curriculum map embedded in the ENGLISH 101 Instructor's Guide based on four learning objectives that embedded library components into six weeks throughout the semester. This map articulated the information literacy instruction learning outcomes beginning with the Freshman (FYE) with benchmarks, milestones and capstone and ending with Senior. As a meaningful road map to expand upon, the university libraries advanced its mission and became an integral player in the First Year Experience Program.

Two librarians were involved in major First Year Experience Program meetings and a more meaningful dialogue ensued. Derived from these meetings, a comprehensive, outcome based objectives emerged for the entire liberal arts foundational course curriculum by Spring 2011. Three major objectives comprised the focus of the University Libraries information literacy instruction program.

With the Libraries' value realized, in the fall of 2011, information literacy instruction was again required for all ENGLISH 101: Writing: Logic and Rhetoric and also required for TRS 201: Faith Seeking Understanding. While Philosophy 201: The Classical Mind and Philosophy 202: The Modern Mind were considered part of the Learning Communities core curriculum, primary resources framed the context of the courses, therefore, information literacy instruction per se was not directly offered.

Fall 2011—Library as a Place: First Year Experience Reading Room

In an effort to provide students with a space to discuss, interact and study in a more relaxed and social manner, the First Year Experience Reading Room was built as a vehicle of the Center for Academic Success.

Weekly FYE teas, a sort of weekly meet and greet, became standard fare. The weekly coffee, tea and cookies was an informal way for students, librarians, faculty and administrators to connect as friendly faces of the university. By the simple task of taking time to ask students about how they are doing, share about ourselves and ask about their research, a face was put on the libraries. And a friendly face at that. The libraries became a comfortable place to ask questions and generally feel part of the commu-

nity. To improve our value a bit more, and to meet the needs of the students for late night study space, the libraries increased its hours to a 24/7 Monday to Thursday schedule.

Students are on the go, and to reach students when they are and where they are, libraries created a mobile website and a variety of online tutorials and LibGuides to enhance student engagement. This was in addition to our availability for research assistance 100 hours a week, via phone, email, web form, text, and instant messaging or appointments for in-person research sessions. Moreover, the Writing Center held satellite office hours in the library during peak times to assist students with their grammar and writing.

Fall 2012—Learning Communities of Practice in action

The Fall 2012 semester brought another vision of the FYE Learning Communities of Practice with a more standardized focus with ENGLISH 101 and TRS 201 Standard LibGuides. Moreover, as a true knowledge management approach to learning, the LC teams formally brought together all those individuals who guide students in their ongoing thinking, learning and advancement of knowledge. With the same students in the learning community for an entire academic year, it was easier to get to know students and become aware of their needs.

The LC Team Members

- *Instructors*: English, Theology, and Philosophy
- *Undergraduate Advisor*: Assigned to each first-year student to facilitate the progress of the student throughout the year. Even exploratory students were placed into a school so that each and every student could be more closely followed to ensure at-risk students received the assistance needed to be successful in their first year.
- *Undergraduate Fellows*: Sophomores, juniors and seniors with excellent academic standing and social acuity act as peer mentors.
- *Embedded Librarian:* Essential to the LC and an active participant in the teaching and learning process.

A FYE website was constructed with each Learning Community specifically outlining the whole team, contact information and photos of Instructors, Undergraduate Advisor, Undergraduate Fellow and Embedded Librarian. The MyCUA Portal, a password protected website created a means to connect, comment, and engage the learning community. With features that provide the opportunity to post directly to Facebook, Blog, Twitter, YouTube, and other social media, the portal became a point of convergence. So with a variety of scrumptious and mouthwatering recipes in our information literacy cookbook CUA's *Sous Chef* Embedded Librarian First Year Experience emerged.

Sous Chef's Recipe for Embedded Librarianship and Information Literacy Learning

As a proponent of the Constructivist Learning Theory, I believe that learning takes place best when individuals are able to find meaning and make sense of their world and thereby create order out of chaos. This means that students gain knowledge and wisdom from their experience of the world. It is important to create context and meaning from the perspective of academic requirements and equally important to engage the student and provide a rich environment for learning. Knowledge and knowledge construction, self-regulated learning and sense making are key components to this approach to teaching and learning. Since students have many different learning styles, offering opportunities for learning in many ways affords the student with a variety of tools and techniques to be successful.

Moreover, dialogue and discourse are the means that negotiate the tension between individual knowledge and social knowledge inherent in this method. In this way, the individual is able to empower themselves and learn individually and in a social context. Metacognition or thinking about thinking occurs when students are endowed with the power to choose not only what they will learn, within a framework of the course requirements, but also how they will learn. To that end the library assignment and the library instruction and learning objects were

TABLE 1. Timeline of Changes in the University Libraries System

Year	Item	Details
2008	Lib Qual+ Satisfaction Survey Undergraduate, Graduate and Faculty	Greatest perceived weakness/adequacy gap : • Print and/or electronic journals • Print materials • Library website usability
	Undergraduate	Perceived weakness: • Convenient hours • Library space
	Graduate	Perceived weakness: • Library space • Modern equipment
	Faculty	Perceived weakness: • Electronic resources • Electronic resources accessible from home or office
	Undergraduate, Graduate and Faculty	Acceptable service: • Visually appealing facility • Giving users individual attention • Instruction • Community space for group and learning • Caring staff
2009	Addition of CUA University Goals for General Education	• Find information • Assess relevance • Legal and ethical use
	Research Guides	• LibGuides roll out
	Camtasia Tutorial	• Students harnessing academic research power (sharp) • Two modules (17 minutes) • In Blackboard • Sharp assignment • Assessment survey • Completed prior to face-face library instruction

	Assessment Outcomes	• 57% Response rate
		• Two focus groups
		  » Too long
		  » Wanted to be able to click thru to specific portions
		  » Liked online feature on library website and Blackboard
		  » Good for new grad students
		  » Well done and professional
		• Faculty 90% response rate
		• ~60% Satisfaction

TABLE 1. Timeline of Changes in the University Libraries System

	Orientation Orientation Extended	• Student resource fair • Library tours • Ref Works and Zotero workshops
2010	FYE Program Launch	• Learning communities established • Liberal arts concentration • Library instruction as needed basis • Two librarians in major meetings • Restructured ENG 101 Rhetoric and Logic
	Four Learning Outcomes in ENG 101 Instructor's Guide	• Assess relevance • Differentiate popular and scholarly • Distinguish sources • Locate materials
	CUA Library Tutorials	• Mullen Library virtual tour • How to Find a Book
	Library components included in syllabus	• Identification and description • Division and classification • Definition and process • Thesis and evidence
	Libraries Website	• Mobile website launched
	Middle States Accreditation	• Successful outcome
2011	Learning Outcomes FYE	• Create a research strategy • Critically evaluate information • Use citations appropriately
	FYE Reading Room Mullen	• Center for academic success tutoring • Library instruction • Group study

	Online Tutorials	• Embedded in LibGuides
		  » Based on instructor's writing prompt
		    * Introduction and keywords
		    * Searching the online catalog #1, and #2
		    * Searching article databases.

	24/7 Hours	• Monday to Thursday with limited services
	Writing Center	• Office hours in library

designed to provide the student with opportunities to reflect on how they can apply their knowledge to their research project.

This Sous Chef was embedded in four learning communities of practice; the ENGLISH 101 LibGuide became the recipe for the students to navigate the terrain. This delicious entrée was designed specifically as a portal for ENGLISH 101 and yet provided flexibility to refine distinctive tastes. The tabs include: choosing the topic, books, journal articles, databases with a subject index, and tutorials gave the students much food for thought.

As a Sous Chef, it was important for me to give the students what they needed to be successful. So I created a recipe card handout that included an outline of the information literacy instruction complete with search examples, screen shots and other possible search terms so that the students had the resources, techniques and best practices for them to use going forward. While the students were whipping up their piece de résistance, they had to make sense of what I was teaching so that they could recreate the recipe as they furthered their research inquiry.

NOTES

1. Oakleaf, Megan, Megan Oakleaf, MLS, PhD http://meganoakleaf.info/.
2. Karagiorgi, Y and Symeou, L. (2005) *Translating Constructivism into Instructional Design: Potential and Limitations.* Educational Technology & Society, 8(1), 17–27.

TABLE 1. Timeline of Changes in the University Libraries System

	Collection Changes	**Print resources** • Popular reading collection added **Electronic resources** • ARTstor • Eighteenth-century collections online • Literature resource

	Library Facility	**Main reading room**
		• 85 Additional outlets added to meet increased laptop use
		• Print periodicals moved to stacks to free up more study group space
		• Comfy chairs added
		• Networked printer/copiers moved next to this space
		Media viewing area
		• Three tv's
		  » Two 32" flat screens
		  » One combo VHS/DVD
		• Blue Ray disk player

	Library Instruction Survey	**50% Response rate**
		• Learned
		  » Sources books and articles
		  » Positive on database searching
		• Liked to learn
		  » More time to practice
		  » Sometimes boring

2012	Libraries Website Spring 2012	• New website with soft launch discovery layer

	Embedded Librarians in FYE Learning Communities Fall 2012	• Standardized ENG 101 and TRS201 LibGuides
		  » Create a research strategy
		  » Critically evaluate information
		  » Use citations appropriately

	ENG101 Survey	**10% Response rate**
		• Learned
		  » How to use the catalog
		  » About article databases
		  » General encyclopedias
		• Like to learn
		  » More on narrowing topic
		  » More on citations
		  » More on newspaper articles
		• 95% Likely to use library

3. Rodriguez, Miranda, "Assessment & Learning Outcomes at CUA a holistic approach." (2012) http://slis.cua.edu/res/docs/symposium/2012-symposium/rodriguez.pdf

4. Shumaker, David. *The Embedded Librarian: Innovative Strategies for Taking Knowledge Where It's Needed.* New Jersey: Information Today, 2012.

5. Catholic University of America, FYE Program, http://firstyear.cua.edu/

6. Catholic University of America Libraries Online Newsletter, http://libraries.cua.edu/newsletter/index.cfm

7. Catholic University of America Libraries, Summon Search Box, http://libraries.cua.edu/

8. Catholic University of America Libraries, ENGLISH 101 LibGuide, http://guides.lib.cua.edu/english101

9. CUA Libraries Online Tutorials, http://guides.lib.cua.edu/content.php?pid=365296&sid=2990380.

10. CUA Libraries Video Tutorials, http://libraries.cua.edu/tutorials/index.cfm.

11. LibQual+ and LibQual Lite, http://www.libqual.org/home

12. CUA Libraries Blog, http://www.lib.cua.edu/wordpress/newsevents/category/general/

13. CUA Center for Academic Success, http://success.cua.edu/

14. Giltrud, Marianne, CUA SLIS Bridging the Spectrum 2011, http://slis.cua.edu/res/docs/giltrud.pdf

15. Giltrud, Marianne, CUA SLIS Bridging the Spectrum 2010, http://slis.cua.edu/

TABLE 1. Timeline of Changes in the University Libraries System

Theology Survey	**50% response rate**
	• Learned
	  » Article databases
	  » Subject encyclopedias
	  » Citations
	• Liked to learn
	  » More on citations
	  » More on Ref Works
	  » More on narrowing search
	• 96% Likely or very likely to use library

Summon Discovery Layer	Launched Spring 2013

res/docs/symposium/2010-symposium/Giltruddigital-ethnography.pdf

16. SCHULTE, S. Embedded Academic Librarianship: A Review of the Literature. Evidence Based Library and Information Practice, North America, 7, Dec. 2012. Available at: <http://ejournals.library.ualberta.ca/index.php/EBLIP/article/view/17466/14528>.

One Ingredient, Many Flavors:
Following One Event through the Information Timeline

Nia Lam, Research & Instruction Librarian, University of Washington Bothell & Cascadia Community College Library, nlam@ uwb.edu; Beth Sanderson, Research & Instruction Librarian, University of Washington Bothell & Cascadia Community College Library, bsanderson@uwb.edu

NUTRITION INFORMATION

This recipe is intended as an introduction to the information timeline (also known as the information cycle) and is especially beneficial to undergraduates (such as students in a composition or history course) who are researching a historical event. The Information Timeline activity helps students understand how knowledge is produced, distributed and shared following an event and across different types of resources. We have used this recipe for lower-division Research Writing classes.

COOKING TIME

- Approximately 30 minutes.
- This activity can take place in any classroom (no computers required). It can be led by an embedded librarian in collaboration with a faculty member.

INGREDIENTS AND EQUIPMENT

- Example of an information timeline/information cycle (handout or website of your choice)
- Examples of primary and secondary sources related to the same event (one for every 2–4 students). The event you choose does not have to be the same

as the event referred to in your example timeline. For example, use a photo of Rosa Parks' arrest as the beginning of your timeline, and then provide other sources like news articles documenting the arrest and biographies of Rosa Parks

- Citations for each source
- Worksheet with questions
- Blue painter's tape

PREPARATION

- Find an example of an information timeline. There are many handouts and websites to choose from on the Internet.
- Gather examples of primary and secondary sources related to the same event.
- Create and print citations for each source on separate strips of paper.
- Create and print worksheet for each group, with questions and directions.
- Place a strip of blue tape on the floor, a long table, or a wall.

THE EMBEDDED PROJECT
Introduction

- Display timeline example and explain how knowledge is produced, distributed, and shared following an event across different types of resources.

- Explain to students that in small groups, they will look at various sources that document the immediate and continuing impact of an event, and they will build their own timeline as a class.
- Show students a photo that represents a historical event (i.e. Rosa Parks arrest photo) and put this photo as the first item on the timeline (blue tape).

Small group activity

- Have students get in groups of 2–4. For each group, give one example source, one citation (that does not match their source), and one worksheet with questions and directions.
- Give students a few minutes to study their source and then answer questions on their worksheet (Figure 1.)

Groups take their handout to the blue tape line that represents the information timeline. They place their source (with citation) on the information timeline in order of date originally published. Instruction librarian checks to make sure all sources are in order. If not, tell the class how many items are out

FIGURE 1. Small Group Activity Worksheet

1. **How long after the event do you think it was published?**
   a. Days
   b. Months
   c. Years

2. **What type of source is this?**
   a. Newspaper article
   b. Scholarly journal article
   c. Book
   d. Reference/encyclopedia source

3. **What database do you think I used to find this?**
   a. UW WorldCat/UW Libraries Catalog
   b. Historical newspaper database like *ProQuest New York Times*
   c. Article database like *JSTOR* or *Google Scholar*
   d. Reference database like *Gale Virtual Reference Library*

4. **Go talk another group.**
   a. Describe your resources to each other. Do the other group members agree with your answers to questions 1–3?
   b. Which one do you think was published first?
   c. Does the other group have the citation that matches your resource? If not, go talk to another group and repeat steps a–c. Continue to talk to other groups until you have found your citation.

5. **Tape or staple your citation here:**

6. **Go place this sheet on the Information Timeline (sheets should be in order of when your resource was first published!)**

of order. Ask volunteers (or one member from each group) to review and rearrange items on the timeline.

Class discussion

Ask each group to describe their source and answer the worksheet questions. Display each source, either a hard copy or electronic copy if there is a projector, as they discuss. Encourage students to think about which types of sources appeared near the beginning of the timeline (i.e. newspaper articles) and which types of sources appeared later (i.e. scholarly journals, books).

ALLERGY WARNINGS

Students are often confused, when looking at citations, about the difference between date published and date accessed. So, while you may think they will easily line up the sources on the timeline according to published date, this is not usually the case. You may want to address this before you begin, or just wait to see how it plays out and use this for an impromptu discussion of citation practices and conventions.

CHEFS' NOTE

The information timeline activity is designed to get students moving around the classroom and talking with each other. It can be a good icebreaker activity, or it could be scheduled as a "middle chunk" of a workshop in order to refresh students if they've been sitting for a period of time.

This recipe could be adapted to a non-historical event. For example, you could have the beginning of the timeline start with a psychology study and use a variety of other sources that reference the psychology study.

ADDITIONAL RESOURCES

Information timeline/ information cycle examples:
- The Information Cycle (University of Washington Libraries): http://guides.lib.washington.edu/content.php?pid=55083&sid=2837441
- The Information Timeline (Meriam Library, California State University Library – Chico): http://library.ndsu.edu/education/files/2009/10/information_timeline_handout.pdf
- Flow of Information (UCLA Library): http://www.library.ucla.edu/libraries/college/flow-information

A Research-Infused Entrée for First-Year Students

Stacey Shah, Distance Learning Librarian, Elgin Community College; Connie James-Jenkin, Elgin Community College, Elgin, IL

NUTRITION INFORMATION

This recipe introduces information literacy instruction and the library to new college students in both the brick and mortar and virtual classrooms and gives them an inviting taste of nourishing college-level research, resources, and guidance from librarians. The project fosters supportive student-librarian relationships to endure through the students' college experience and beyond.

SERVES

60+ classes, each with approximately 25 students

COOKING TIME

8 weeks

INGREDIENTS AND EQUIPMENT

- Access to the Learning Management System (LMS)
- Tutorial software (this project used Captivate/YouTube)
- Video camera or smartphone
- LibGuides
- Receptive teaching faculty and administration
- Helpful instructional technologists
- Team of dedicated and adventurous librarians

PREPARATION

- Secure the support of administration and teaching faculty involved with planning and coordinating first-year seminar classes and curriculum (COL 101 at Elgin)
- Collaborate to determine a common class reading and develop an associated chapbook project assignment requiring research and use of library resources
- Attend first-year seminar instructor orientation and answer questions regarding the assignment research component
- Work with instructional technologists to embed librarians in the LMS course site for each seminar section
- Create a "Library and Research Help" topic and "Ask a Librarian" discussion forum in each LMS course site
- Train librarians on best practices for working within the LMS environment

COOKING METHOD

Students are introduced to a common reading and the requirements of their chapbook assignment prior to visiting the library for their instruction session. They are required to select four words or ideas from their reading to research. They must have at least one library resource for each of their four words/ideas. Ultimately, they will use their research to inform the creation of a chapbook. The chapbook can take on any number of different forms including written word, art, collage, video, music, etc. but must contain four words from the reading and information about the sources used to research the words.

Each class has its own embedded librarian to guide in research process throughout the duration of the class. The librarians introduce themselves through the LMS in a dedicated discussion forum for library and research help and prepare students for their in-class library instruction session. During the in-class session, librarians introduce students to college-level resources ad guide them in explore the best resources for their chapbook project and documenting their research process by having them fill out a worksheet.

Once the in-class session ends, the librarian's instruction and guidance continues through the LMS course site. Students can interact with and get help from the librarian through the dedicated discussion forum. The librarian continues to post links to recommend resources, video tutorials, and images to guide in the research process, and links to the class LibGuide. The librarian also answers any posted student question and the whole class benefits from viewing the answers.

ALLERGY WARNINGS

- This assignment requires a great deal of collaboration between the seminar instructors and librarians. It is important for instructors to adequately prepare their students for the library session by introducing them to the common reading and assignment requirements. If they do not, librarians may have to take up valuable class time explaining the assignment.
- Managing librarians embedded in a large number of classes requires a lot of oversight, availability for troubleshooting, and strong teamwork between librarians and instructional technologists.
- Having two librarians embedded in each class allows for a "back-up" librarian to answer questions and provide assistance in cases where the lead librarian is unavailable. This provides for more efficient service and instruction.

CHEFS' NOTE

At the end of the eight-week course, each class displayed their best chapbooks in a gallery walk, and the librarians had the opportunity to see the end products. The results were astounding. The students used a variety of library resources to create imaginative, thoughtful projects including music compositions, collages, journals, and videos. Because the students were required to do library research for their chapbook project, they were much more invested in the library instruction than in past semesters. By embedding librarians in the classes and allowing them to work with the students throughout the eight weeks of class, librarians were able to develop a much more involved relationship with the students and guide them thoughout the entire process of creating their chapbook. This research-infused entrée made for a very satisfying meal.

Librarian Prescription

Caroline Conley, Information Literacy Librarian, cconley@shoreline.edu; Claire Murata, Faculty Librarian, cmurata@shoreline. edu, Shoreline Community College

NUTRITION INFORMATION
This librarian recipe works at the reference desk or in face-to-face classroom: in face-to-face instruction, students come to the reference desk to fill out a librarian prescription (LP) with a librarian's help. In an online classroom: online classes receive an example completed LP that they emulate, filling in their topics, keywords and research findings. The purposes are for the students to: identify keywords from their topic; use those keywords to implement a search strategy using appropriate sources; find research sources aimed at a specific information need determined by their topic; and understand the usefulness of interacting with a librarian for research help. We use this for Chemistry and English but it is designed to be multi-disciplinary.

SERVES
30–60 students depending on the capacity of the reference desk and capacity for grading the LPs

COOKING TIME
Each interaction with a librarian can take anywhere from 10–30 minutes, depending on the student's needs, and whether the interaction is face-to-face or an asynchronous online interaction.

INGREDIENTS AND EQUIPMENT
- Computer
- Blank LP's
- Example LP's

PREPARATION
Students receive instruction in the form of a workshop or tutorials that give them instruction and background on how to identify keywords and how to use appropriate research resources. This project assumes an assigned, specific research project, such as a research paper.

The librarian creates a paper form that has a list of resources with checkboxes, divided by reference, books, articles, and style guides. There is space for the librarian to jot down the student's thesis or topic, space for brainstorming keywords and search strings, and space to jot down call numbers, websites and Libguides. There is also space for the librarian's signature and date. Contact information for the library is also helpful.

COOKING METHOD
Students are required to visit a reference desk on their own for a reference interview in which they can brainstorm topics, refine their topic, identify keywords and search strings, and get specific resources that

might be appropriate for their topic. Students leave the desk with a librarian prescription, a form on which the librarian has recorded the main points of the reference interview so the student walks away from the desk with a research plan. The librarian signs and dates the prescription so the students can show their instructor and receive credit. Some instructors assign the librarian prescription as an assignment, and some assign it for extra credit, but we recommend requiring credit for the students to invest in the assignment.

In the online variation, students receive a sample, completed LP. The student then drafts their own LP, which they send to the librarian, who, in turn, adds keywords, search strings, and appropriate resources. The librarian may also write extra comments about the student's topic and research process.

ALLERGY WARNING
This assignment can overwhelm the reference desk. We sometimes staff the desk with three librarians before a prescription is due. More than one librarian may need to respond to librarian prescriptions for an online course. Unless the directions are clear, students will sometimes complete their

research before they approach the desk for a prescription, believing they only need a signature. If students have received much research instruction in the past, they can feel it unnecessary to work with a librarian. Our library instruction program limits the librarian prescription assignment to two disciplines, although any student who requests research help will get one as a record of the reference interaction.

CHEFS' NOTE

Most students are surprised at the level of support once they come to the reference desk for research help. Many times they need to talk through their anxiety and they respond with relief to reassurances of help and support from an expert who does not grade. Many students will not give themselves permission to go to the reference desk without the requirement from their instructor. While anecdotal response is positive, implications for future assessment include getting written feedback from students about satisfaction with the assignment, and whether the assignment encourages them to return to the desk on their own.

FIGURE 1. Librarian prescription for a Cesar Chavez research

LIBRARIAN PRESCRIPTION

Shoreline Community College library@shoreline.edu
REFERENCE DESK: 206 546-6939 | WEB SITE: http://shoreline.libguides.com/home

Date:

Course and Instructor:

"TAKE 2 ASPIRIN AND CHAT WITH US IN THE MORNING"
Live Librarian Help: AskWA http://bit.ly/PZ8qiF

1 ENCYCLOPEDIAS & BACKGROUND

☐ A-Z Maps
☐ CQ Researcher
☑ Encyclopedia Of Human Rights
☑ Gale Virtual Reference Library*
☐ Literature Resource Center*
☐ Medlineplus.gov
☐ Oxford English Dictionary
☐ Opposing Viewpoints *
☐ Sirs
☐ WOIS

2 BOOKS & EBOOKS
☑ SCC Catalog
☑ Ebrary
☐ Worldcat.Org
☐ Google Books

3 ARTICLES & DATABASES
☑ Academic Search Complete
☐ Proquest
☑ JSTOR
☐ Google Scholar
☐ Abi/Inform Trade And Industry
☐ Artstor
☐ Cinahl Plus
☐ Eric
☐ New York Times Historical
☐ Pubmed
☐ PsycArticles
☐ Versus Law

LEARNING GUIDES
http://shoreline.libguides.com/

CITATIONS
http://shoreline.libguides.com/citation

Ray Howard Library @ Shoreline Community College

Research Topic:

How Cesar Chavez contributed to food justice in the United States.

Search Keywords and Search Strings:

"Cesar Chavez" AND "food justice"
"Cesar Chavez" AND "distributive justice"
"Cesar Chavez AND poverty
"Cesar Chavez" AND pesticides
"food justice" AND agriculture

Book Call Numbers and Web Sites:

"Why Cesar Chavez Led a Movement as well as a Union" article (Academic Search Complete)

Justice and Natural Resources: Concepts, Strategies and Applications (ebrary)

Food Justice Certified at http://www.agriculturaljusticeproject.org/home.html (website)

Notes:

Finding the right keywords to search with can be tricky. People use differing words to describe the same thing. Like "pop" and "soda"

While searching Academic Search Complete, I saw that one of the subject words (like a keyword) was "distributive justice" so I tried searching with that and it gave me great results!

Librarian Signature and date

04/16/2013 Caroline Conley

* KCLS - King County Library - www.kcls.org ** SPL - Seattle Public Library - www.spl.org Sno-Isle Libraries www.sno-isle.org

3. Everyday Meals: Adaptable Instructions for Embedded Projects

We know that every library is different. The Everyday Meals section highlights projects that can be adapted to a variety of settings. These embedded instruction techniques have been utilized in multiple learning environments and in libraries with staff varying from one librarian to dozens of subject specialists. If you are looking for a collection of go-to techniques for a burgeoning embedded instructional program, start here.

Cooking Up Collaboration!
Faculty-Librarian Collaboration in Online Instruction

Melissa Langridge, User Education Coordinator, Niagara University, mlangridge@niagara.edu; Kristin Burger, Adjunct Instructor, Niagara University, burger.kristin@gmail.com; Blake Carver, Owner, LIS Host, btcarver@lisnews.com; Natalie Bennett, Outreach Librarian , Niagara University Library, nbennett@niagara.edu

NUTRITION INFORMATION

This recipe demonstrates how, through a partnership approach with faculty, comprehensive library instruction can be provided online for students in a meaningful and integrated way.

Instruction librarians have found that students' information literacy skills obtained in freshman English composition courses do not always transfer when conducting research within a specific discipline; most faculty would likely agree. The development of this lesson began when a history professor expressed concern that students cannot successfully complete writing assignments in a college-level history course without knowing how to identify sources, reference a secondary source, and analyze a primary source. However, it is difficult to schedule time in the library within a survey course. Not only is there an overabundance of history to cover in a short time, but introductory courses are usually too large for the standard library instruction computer lab.

SERVES
Unlimited

COOKING TIME

Students had one week to complete a library assignment early in the semester. However, the post test was given at the end of the semester after the completion of two course assignments in order to assess knowledge gained through the practical application of library resources.

INGREDIENTS AND EQUIPMENT

- University of Arizona Guide On The Side open source software
- Course-specific library assignment
- Online survey
- Rubric
- Computer access

PREPARATION

In advance of the session:
- Meet with course instructor in order to tailor information literacy instruction to course
- Secure assistance from IT specialist/ systems librarian in order to manage required software
- Administer pretest to students in order to assess prior knowledge and obtain baseline

COOKING METHOD

The use of active learning in library teaching provides students with the opportunity to practice using the skills they're learning in an engaging way. Guide on the Side is open source software that was developed by the University of Arizona. This software allows librarians to develop customized information literacy tutorials. These interactive tutorials run in a frame alongside a live website, such as the Library's home page. Students follow the librarian's step-by-step instructions in order to actively complete the tutorial. This is a great alternative to passively viewing an online demonstration video. This software applies the same teaching philosophy already held in the physical library classroom where students learn by doing.

Step 1: Present relevant discussion topic to students in order to place research in context:

Did American intervention in World War II get us out of the Great Depression?

Students learned in class that American intervention in World War II was a major factor in getting the U.S. out of the Great Depression. The professor challenged them to find proof of this assertion using both primary and secondary research from credible sources. Additionally, students explained their rationale in the selection of sources used as evidence.

Step 2: Students will be exposed to the following resources through the librarian creation of Guide on the Side tutorials:

- Primary research:
  - » Google
  - » New York Times Historical database (or other historical news database)
- Secondary research:
  - » JSTOR (or database of your choice)

You can add multiple choice questions to test student learning as they progress through each tutorial. However, only the quizzes embedded at the end of each tutorial are available for assessment.

Step 3: Upon the completion of the three tutorials, students will complete the course library assignment (Figure 1) for a homework grade to ensure completion.

This assignment was created for a few reasons. First, it was a way for students to practice finding and using appropriate resources for the upcoming course assignments. Second, the professor figured it was a way to introduce students to meeting her expectations and course requirements. A rubric was created for the library assignment that was modeled on the rubric used for the two course papers, thus making clear the expectations for both research and analysis. Once

these criteria have been established, there was no reason why the students would not do well on the first major course assignment.

FIGURE 1. HIS 199 Library Assignment:

Question: Did American intervention in World War II get us out of the Great Depression?

Initial Response:

Find Supporting Evidence:

1. Describe the type of primary source you found:
   a. Why did you choose this primary source? What makes it better than the other results?
   b. What resource did you use to find this source?
2. Find one newspaper article from the time the event occurred:
   a. Citation:
   b. Why did you choose this article?
   c. What resource did you use to find this source?
3. Find one academic source that provides insight into this event.
   a. Citation:
   b. Why did you choose this article?
   c. What resource did you use to find this source?
4. In a paragraph, respond to the question again, but support your statements using the library research you found as evidence: Did American intervention in World War II get us out of the Great Depression?
5. Detailed Response:

ALLERGY WARNINGS

The library assignment is given early in the semester as preparation for two major course assignments given during the course of one semester. Each assignment provided should build on the same information skills each time, thus, there is a realistic opportunity to change student skills into learned behaviors. The students who leave papers until the last minute often have trouble identifying sources. Create a webpage/handout reminding them of the difference between primary and secondary sources, library resources to use in the discipline and librarian contact information. Also, because the post test is given at the end of the semester, anticipate less participants than the pretest. Discuss with the professor ways to increase this number such as adding extra credit to their final assignment.

CHEFS' NOTE

Once set up, Guide on the Side software is very easy to use. Student response to the interactivity of the Guide on the Side tutorials was positive. Faculty-librarian collaboration is key to the success of assigning IL online or ongoing assessment of the development of information literacy in students. The professor stated that after the completion of the online library assignment the quality of scholarly research increased, students' cited sources seemed to be relevant and in support of their arguments. In general, student grades increased due to the appropriate use of library resources.

ADDITIONAL RESOURCES

- Guide on the Side http://code.library.arizona.edu/gots/

Five Shakes at Information Literacy

Sara Klink, Assistant Director of Library Services, Stark State College, sklink@starkstate.edu; Melissa Bauer, Online Learning Librarian, Kent State University, mbauer10@kent.edu

NUTRITION INFORMATION

The purpose of this project is to give students exposure to the research process through embedded instruction sessions. Moving away from the one-shot session allows students time to reflect and strengthen the skills taught to them about the research process. Each 30-minute mini-session incorporates research information and active learning activities. Students will use Glogster, a free tool for creating posters online, to showcase and share their own research process. Glogster allows users to add text, live links, post pictures, upload documents and more. The tool is a visually appealing and effective way to incorporate active learning within library instruction.

COOKING TIME

5 weeks or until done.

INGREDIENTS AND EQUIPMENT

- Glogster account
- Access to computer with Internet for instructor and each student

PREPARATION

- Collaborate with faculty member before semester begins to plan library research sessions over the course of the semester

FIGURE 1. A student's research process, as illustrated using Glogster

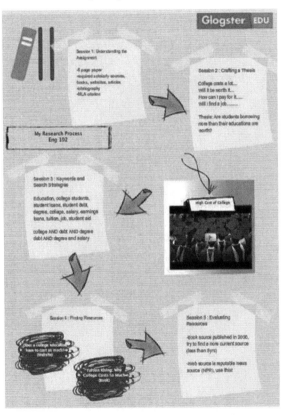

- Plan content and delivery for the five mini-research sessions (20 minutes each)
  - » Session 1: Understanding the assignment/students set-up Glogs
  - » Session 2: Finding a topic/crafting a thesis

- » Session 3: Choosing keywords and developing search strategies
- » Session 4: Search library resources, catalog, databases, etc.
- » Session 5: Evaluating the sources
- Create student Glogster accounts

COOKING METHOD

The mini-sessions will be incorporated for the length of the project. Each 30 minute session needs to be taught in a classroom with student computers. During each session, students will be creating corresponding sections on their Glogs. For example, Session 2 has students developing a thesis statement. After students craft a thesis, they will add it to their individual Glog.

- Session 1: Understanding the assignment/Students set-up Glogs
  - » Librarian delivers instruction; reviews assignment and expectations (scholarly resources, number of sources, timeline, etc.)
  - » Students create individual Glogs, choose background, title, etc.

- Session 2: Finding a topic/crafting a thesis
  - » Librarian delivers instruction on selecting an appropriate research topic.

» Students will brainstorm and list possible topics on their Glogs.
» Students will use their selected topic and formulate a thesis statement or research question. This will be done on their Glogs.

- Session 3: Choosing keywords and developing search strategies
  » Librarian delivers instruction on finding keywords and developing search strategies.
  » Students will identify possible keywords and phrases from their individual thesis/research question and add them to their Glogs.

- Session 4: Search library resources, catalog, databases, etc.
  » Librarian delivers overview of research tools, such as the catalog, databases, and websites.
  » Students will practice searching resources using keywords identified in session 3.
  » Students will list or link all sources (books, articles, websites) to their Glogs.

- Session 5: Evaluating the sources
  » Librarian delivers instruction on source evaluation.
  » Students will apply evaluation criteria to sources and add findings to their Glogs.
  » Session Wrap-Up
  » Students can upload notes, outline and final copy of their papers/projects to their Glogs.

ALLERGY WARNINGS

- Glogster is a free online tool that may change/update frequently, make sure to review tool prior to each use. We recommend using Glogster.edu to limit advertisements on the page.
- In Session 1 give students enough time to become familiar with Glogster. Have students practice creating content, choosing backgrounds and uploading documents or images.
- During Session 5 some students may find that some or many of their sources did not pass the evaluation criteria. Be prepared to assist in those cases or allow students extra time for questions.

CHEFS' NOTE

Students enjoy doing something creative while learning about the research process. This project allows for a great deal of collaboration with instructors. It can be modified to fit any research project.

Librarians and instructors teaching online can also adapt this recipe. The 5 mini-sessions can be held in a variety of formats. In online environments they could be taught in an online, synchronous learning space, recorded and shown as a video or tutorial or shown in conjunction with a live discussion. Students could then add their content to their Glogs and submit their individual Glog for the instructor or librarian's review.

ADDITIONAL RESOURCES

- Glogster http://edu.glogster.com/
- LibGuide URL http://libguides.stark.kent.edu/glogster

iMovie, MS PowerPoint, ProShow Producer, Oh My!
Helping Students Find the Right Path to Creating Meaningful Digital Projects.

Steve Dresbach, Technology Instructor, Milne Library, SUNY Geneseo, Geneseo, NY, dresbach@geneseo.edu; Maria Perpetua Socorro U. Liwanag, Assistant Professor Reading/Literacy, SUNY Geneseo, Geneseo, NY, liwanag@geneseo.edu; Michelle Costello, Education and Instructional Design Librarian, SUNY Geneseo, Geneseo, NY, costello@geneseo.edu

NUTRITION INFORMATION

This recipe is designed as a demonstration of the software applications iMovie, MS PowerPoint and ProShow Producer as students create a book trailer assignment for an undergraduate education course using one of the three pieces of software. The purpose is to introduce students to software they can use to create a book trailer or other digital projects. Understanding how software presentation tools can be used in the classroom and when to use the appropriate tools enables pre-service teachers to better address the use of new literacies in their teaching.

SERVES

20–30 students

COOKING TIME

Cooking time is 110 minutes, two 50 minute sessions to cover the three software titles

INGREDIENTS AND EQUIPMENT

- Computer access for all students
- Instructor's station
- Access to software applications

PREPARATION

A library or subject guide should be created for students in the class. The guide would contain information about copyright and book trailers and how to create them (including videos). It would also include links to websites for finding images and music for digital projects (such as book trailers). Students should have an understanding of what a book trailer is and have seen examples. Additionally, create a short book trailer of a young adult book (with each piece of software) using images, text, and audio to use in the session.

COOKING METHOD
Part One

As class begins a discussion is started to get students thinking of what they will need to consider as they begin to create a book trailer (i.e. finding related images & audio and how to integrate text, images, and sound to convey the intended message).

Part Two

Instructor plays the (three) book trailers they created, mentioning the software used to create each one. After viewing the trailers instructor leads a brief discussion on the differences noticed in each of the book trailers.

Part Three

Instructor gives a brief demonstration for each software title (iMovie, ProShow Producer and MS PowerPoint) looking at the user interface and some of the techniques required to create a book trailer, including adding and enhancing images, text, audio, animations & Ken Burns effect and transitions. Lastly, students are shown how to export their book trailers into a standard video format such as QuickTime.

Students are encouraged throughout to seek help with the software outside of class time.

ALLERGY WARNING

Students may need follow-up consultations after the workshop as there isn't enough time to cover the software in its entirety.

CHEFS' NOTE

This session works best if the instructor doesn't try to cover the software in great detail and everything required to create a book trailer. The instruction is primarily to give an overview of the book trailer creation process and give an awareness of what the software can do so that students can intelligently choose the software they want to use for their project. Students are expected to seek help outside of class if needed with the instructor or digital media lab staff.

INSTRUCTIONAL RESOURCES
- Digital media lab professional and student staff in Milne Library

Roman Pancake Tart à la Library:
A Multi-Layered Approach to Integrating Library Instruction into a Classical Studies Course

Chanitra Bishop, Instruction and Emerging Technologies Librarian, Indiana University Bloomington, chbishop@indiana.edu;
Catherine Minter, Ph.D., Arts and Humanities Librarian, Indiana University Bloomington, cjminter@indiana.edu

NUTRITION INFORMATION
This is an authentic Roman recipe with two essential components: ragout (aka course syllabus) and pancakes (aka instruction sessions).[1]

Place a pancake in a circular baking dish. Spoon the ragout over the pancake, cover it with another, and repeat until the ingredients are used up. Make a little hole in the final pancake and insert a straw (aka assessment) to serve as a chimney through which steam can escape during cooking.

This recipe describes a layered approached to library instruction. The lessons start with more basic information that is familiar to students and build to more complex library information.

SERVES
Optimum: 20–25 students. Humanities: Classical Studies

COOKING TIME
Varies depending on class needs. Cooking time is 120 to 200 minutes or four 30–50 minute sessions.

INGREDIENTS AND EQUIPMENT
- Subject-specific websites frequently used within the discipline, for example *Perseus Digital Library, Homer Multitext, Stoa Consortium* projects, *Voice of the Shuttle: Classical Studies*
- Computers with Internet access
- Website Evaluation Worksheet (one copy for each group)

PREPARATION
Collaborate—Meet with the instructor to learn instructor expectations and explain lesson plan and activities. Explore ways to involve the instructor in the session by encouraging the instructor to share why resources are important or how they use the resources. Find out major topics to be discussed in class and incorporate them into your instruction sessions. If necessary, revise lesson plan based on instructor goals.

Work with professor to determine cooking time and temperature. Your sessions need to be long enough to really cook! Remember a properly planned session can lead to rave reviews from students and professors asking for seconds!

Be Your Own Chef (BYOC)—The lesson plan is flexible; customize the lesson plan based on the course goals and needs of the instructor and students.

Check your pantry (library collections) to make sure you have all the necessary ingredients (print and electronic resources) before you start cooking.

COOKING METHOD
Pancake Layer 1: Discipline-Based Website Evaluation
Students often use websites to conduct research but are often unaware of subject-specific websites used in their discipline. This session aims to introduce them to these sites and differences between them, and to teach them to evaluate the effectiveness and usefulness of each site.

Learning Outcome:
- Students will become familiar with key websites used in their discipline and learn to evaluate the websites and when to use them.

Directions:
Open session with a 3–5 minute discussion on criteria for evaluating websites. Ask students how they distinguish a "good" website from a "bad" website.

Divide students into groups, by rows works well. Assign each group a website to review. Give each group 15–20 minutes to review the assigned website and provide an analysis of the website based on their judgment and referring to questions from the website evaluation worksheet.

After students have reviewed the websites, ask each group to present the website analysis to the class. Discuss the pros and cons of each website and make a grid with the results.

Pancake Layer 2: Sources for Background Research
This session introduces students to tools for background research: general and subject-specific encyclopedias.

Learning Outcomes:
- Students will understand the differences between general and subject-specific encyclopedias (and also between traditional and non-traditional encyclopedias), including drawbacks and benefits of each type.
- Students will gain an understanding of the purpose of using a variety of sources for background information and are introduced to subject-specific encyclopedias that are used in their discipline.

- Students will see the benefit of doing background research and using sources in addition to *Wikipedia* to explore a topic.

Ingredients:
- General and subject-specific encyclopedias, both print and online. Examples of the former include *Wikipedia* and *Encyclopedia Britannica*; examples of the latter include *The Oxford Classical Dictionary*, *Oxford Reference Online*, *The Classic Tradition* and *Brill's New Pauly: Encyclopedia of the Ancient World*.
- Computers with Internet access to allow students to use different encyclopedias
- Encyclopedia Evaluation Worksheet (one copy for each group)

Directions:
Divide students into groups, by rows works well. Assign each group two encyclopedias to review: a general encyclopedia and a subject-specific encyclopedia. Ask students to review the same article in the two encyclopedias. Choose a topic relevant to their course assignment(s).

Give students approximately 20 minutes to review the articles. After students have reviewed the articles, discuss the results. Ask each group to share its results and make a grid with the benefits and drawbacks of each encyclopedia as a class.

FIGURE 1. Website Evaluation Worksheet

1. What type of information can you find on this website? What subjects/topics are discussed? Are there articles on the website?

2. Are there inaccuracies in the information? Does it seem to go against received opinion? Does it contain information similar to what you have found in other sources such as encyclopedias or are discussing in class?

3. Who is the publisher? What is the source of the information? Is the information supported by references to other information sources?

4. Is the information presented objectively? Is there evidence of ideological bias?

5. Is the material well written and presented/organized?

6. How does the information relate to your research topic or questions? Would you use this website to do research? If so, when? To learn more about the topic? To find more detailed scholarly information on the topic? How appropriate is the information to your purposes?

Pancake Layer 3: Effective Subject Searching

Now that students have an understanding of the purpose of various reference resources and when to use them, they are ready to begin doing more in-depth research. This session aims to teach students how to conduct effective searches in the library catalog, or indeed any library database.

Learning Outcomes:
- Students will learn how to use the library catalog and/or library databases to retrieve relevant items on a given topic.
- Students will understand the differences between natural language and controlled vocabulary searching, and the ways they influence search results.

Ingredients:
- Computers with Internet access
- Library catalog or any library database
- Search topics based on course content/assignments
- Subject Searching Worksheet, one copy for each group (Figure 2.)

Directions:
Demonstrate a keyword search in the library catalog/database. Choose a sample topic that generates a significant number of irrelevant results. Use one relevant record to demonstrate the use of subject headings (catalog) or subject descriptors (database).

Divide students into groups. Assign each group a topic. Ask students to find at least two relevant books on their assigned topic. They should describe their search steps and any difficulties they encounter.

Give students approximately 15 minutes to complete this exercise. Ask each group to share its results.

Pancake Layer 4: Evaluating Secondary Sources

One of the most challenging tasks in research is deciding whether a secondary source is not only appropriate, but also whether it is relevant to your topic. This session aims to introduce students to the thought processes involved in this activity.

Learning Outcomes:
- Students will understand the differences between scholarly and non-scholarly information, and be able to identify likely examples of both types.
- Students will be able to identify secondary sources that are likely to be relevant to a given topic, basing their judgments on evaluation of library catalog records (for books) and analysis of abstracts (for articles).

Ingredients:
- Sample topic based on course content/assignment
- Library catalog records for several books, scholarly and popular
- Abstracts of several articles, scholarly and popular
- Source Evaluation Worksheet (one copy for each group)

Directions:
Introduce the class to the sample research topic for this exercise and divide the students into several small groups. Assign each group either three or more library catalog records or three or more abstracts of articles.
Ask each group to examine the information in the records/abstracts and evaluate each source 1) as to its appropriateness as a research source, and 2) as to its likely relevance to the sample research topic. Each group should decide which record/abstract seems to point to the most appropriate and relevant secondary source. Ask each group to share its findings and explain its decision processes.

FIGURE 2. Subject Searching Worksheet

1. Did you search by keyword or by subject?

2. Did you use the catalog's advanced search function?

3. How many results did your search retrieve?

4. Were you happy with the first set of results, or did you need to modify your search? If so, what steps did you take?

5. Were you able to find the subject heading(s) used in the catalog to describe your topic?

6. Were you able to explore related works on the same topic?

FIGURE 3. Source Evaluation Worksheet

For books and articles:
1. Who is the author? What are his/her credentials? Does this person seem qualified to write on this topic? Have they written on similar topics?

2. Who is the publisher? Is it an institution, or an individual? If an institution, what are its credentials? Is the source self-published?

3. Does the record/abstract indicate that other secondary sources are referred to in this one (in a bibliography, list of references, etc.)?

4. When was the source published? Does currency of information matter for this topic?

For books:
1. Based on the catalog record, in what ways does this book seem to pertain to this research topic?

2. Does the title seem appropriate to the topic? Do the subject headings seem relevant? Is there a table of contents?

For articles:
1. In what type of periodical does this article appear? Is it a newspaper, a magazine, or a research journal? Who is the target audience?

2. Based on the abstract, in what ways does this article seem to pertain to this research topic?

3. Does the abstract indicate that the arguments used in the article are sound? Is there any evidence of unsubstantiated bias?

4. Does the abstract describe the author's conclusions? Do the author's arguments sound like they would support these conclusions?

CHEFS' NOTE

Course assignments (and concomitant student motivation) are an essential part of this recipe: think of them as the eggs that bind all the ingredients in the layered tart together, both ragout (course content) and pancakes (instruction sessions). Without them, your instruction sessions will not be adequately embedded; and your tart will fall apart.

Incorporate some form of assessment into each of your instruction sessions—for example, worksheets such as those included in this recipe. Remember that assessment can serve the same function as the little straw that is inserted into the Roman pancake tart: to allow steam to escape during cooking!

NOTES
1. Recipe adapted from: Patrick Faas, *Around the Roman Table* (New York: Palgrave Macmillan, 2003), 319–21.

ALLERGY WARNINGS

Choose sample topics for your demonstrations and class activities that allow you to maintain flexibility. Choose topics that support the course syllabus, but aren't necessarily tied to it on a week-by-week level (since it's easy to fall out of step with these). Both faculty and students in the humanities may have a tendency to think that too many cooks spoil the broth! Humanities faculty and students alike tend to be accustomed to a "lone researcher" model and may perceive group activities as inferior or basic; faculty may show a preference for traditional, direct teaching methods as opposed to learner-centered ones. Be aware of these potential prejudices and preferences, and allow for flexibility in your techniques.

Telling Stories about the Library:
Using Photo-Comics as Student Research Narratives

Matt Upson, Director of Undergraduate Library Services, Oklahoma State University, matthewupson@gmail.com;
Alex Mudd, Assistant Professor, Reference and Instruction, Emporia State University, amudd@emporia.edu

NUTRITION INFORMATION

This assignment combines the potential metacognitive and deep learning benefits of reflective exercises with the creative engagement of a multi-media project. We asked students in our information literacy classes to script, design, construct, and share photo-comic narratives utilizing an iPad app. Students reflected on their understanding of and success with the various components of the research process, and identified ways to improve their research skills. Additionally, these comics can be a great way for students to demonstrate multimodal literacy skills and provide feedback on instruction in a humorous and informal manner.

COOKING TIME

- Instructors should spend an hour or two practicing with the app and creating their own comic. Plan on spending half an hour or so (depending on the number of students involved) prior to class downloading the app to the individual iPads. Be sure to test out iPad/projector VGA connection prior to session.
- Ten to fifteen minutes should be dedicated to providing a tutorial on how to operate the app.

- Depending on the length of comic, plan on 1–3 hours to prepare the script, take photos and create comic. Students ideally should have their script written and approved prior to working with the iPad and app.
- Plan on spending a few minutes per iPad after the session to save the files to Dropbox or sync with iTunes.

INGREDIENTS AND EQUIPMENT

- iPad(s) with camera.
- App dedicated to creating photo comics. Comic Life ($4.99 through iTunes) is our preferred app, which can be licensed across five devices, although if you are using institutional iPads, you may be required to purchase one app per iPad
- Dropbox or iTunes account belonging to instructor or institution.
- Dropbox app (recommended, not necessary).
- Student-generated script for the comic.
- Keyboard for iPad (recommended to drastically reduce the time needed for the assignment).
- VGA Adaptor for iPad and projector (recommended for improving efficiency of app tutorial)

COOKING METHOD

Digital Storytelling

PREPARATION

This assignment is best implemented after students have received instruction on and have participated in the research process.

- Instructor and students should read through the "Getting Started" manual that is included with the app.
- Instructor should create a sample comic for students to view.
- Instructor should use a VGA adapter to project their iPad screen and provide a brief tutorial on how to use the app.

THE EMBEDDED PROJECT

1. The instructor provides an explanation of the purpose and utility of the assignment. Maybe a dumbed-down version of this: Narrative is an excellent way to allow students to reflect upon their experiences and gain valuable insight into how to improve upon the process as they grow intellectually. By combining the narrative function with the multimodal utility of the comic, students are obliged to create a combination of textual and visual meaning and connect

specific actions and behaviors to the narrative flow.

2. Students prepare a script for the comic based on their own reflection on the various parts of the research process (topic identification and development, searching, evaluation, citation, etcetera). This allows them to arrange a narrative and plan how to visually complement and explain their text narrative. At our institution, we ask students to create a five-page comic that addresses the parts of the research process listed above, as well as an overall assessment of their understanding of the process. The script may (and probably should) be completed outside of class.

   • Scripts are written similarly to a play, with each "panel" of the comic defined and described with visual and textual components. Drafts should be reviewed by instructor to ensure intelligibility and consistency. It is important to emphasize the need for excellent summarization skills on the part of the students. Since there is limited space within a panel for dialogue, students must be sure to highlight the most essential parts of their experience, and not fill the comic with "fluff." Still, you want them to be able to express themselves in a creative and humorous manner, so a balance between content and presentation is vital. Explain that the page and panel content is flexible, so if they have dialogue that is important to them, but may

be too long, they can adjust the number of panels, or add a text only panel to help include the content that they want to share. There is no set template that they must adhere to. They should have the freedom to tell their story without too much constraint, but should also be aware of the necessity for thrift and focus.

3. Students use their scripts as a guide to begin taking photos. Creativity is key here and the photos can be as concrete or as abstract as a student wants, as long as they can defend the connection between text and image. Photos can be automatically saved to the default photo app on the iPad or can be added on the fly directly to the comic.

4. Students open the Comic Life app and create a new comic. They can choose from a blank page or multiple templates and styles. Comics are automatically saved on the device and can be returned to at a later time. If this is the case, it is useful to keep track of which student used which device.

5. Depending on your library's tech setup, comics can be printed, emailed, shared to Twitter or Facebook, or (our preferred option) sent as a PDF to a Dropbox or iTunes account. Using the Dropbox app, we sign in using our personal or institutional account and can upload the PDF directly via wireless network. PDF files can also be saved by synching the iPad to iTunes and saving the file directly to your desktop.

FIGURE 1. Student-generated script for a comic

```
PAGE ONE - A focus on topic development and overall reflection.
Panel One: This panel shows a picture of me slumped over on a desk next to a
computer.

Matt (voiceover): Ughhh. Research might be the most difficult thing ever.

Panel Two: A picture of me sitting at a desk reading through books on the
Civil War. I still look frustrated.

Matt (voiceover): I had a topic for my UL100 class. It was the Civil War and
Religion. I thought it was a good topic, but apparently, that's not specific
enough. I had to think about how to focus the topic by coming up with synonyms
and even changing my topic into a thesis statement or question. My question
ended up being: "how did evangelical Christianity help spark the Civil War?"

Panel Three: Sitting at the computer, but now I'm smiling.

Matt: It's amazing how much easier my research was once I developed a clear
topic and was able to begin searching. Although I had a tough time figuring out
what my initial question would be, I figured out how to make it more specific by
focusing on "evangelical Christianity" instead of just "religion" and I wanted
to look specifically at how it helped start the Civil War. By narrowing my
question, I will have more luck finding resources that I need.
```

6. Students may present their comic as a physical or digital artifact, describing why they have chosen particular images and text to represent their reflection on the research process. Classmates can provide feedback and ask questions.

7. Instructor should erase photos from iPad to ensure student privacy.

8. Instructor should sign out of Dropbox and/or iTunes (if iPad is regularly circulated).

FIGURE 2. Sample panels from student-created comic about the research project

ALLERGY WARNINGS

There is a potential lack of security if Dropbox or iTunes is left synched/logged in and the learning curve on ComicLife app may prevent students from completing the assignment within the allotted time.

CHEFS' NOTE

This assignment can be adapted and used as a one-shot library tour session. Provide your students with iPads and a quick ten-minute tutorial on the app. Then, take them on a short walking tour of your library, providing a basic overview of services. Students can take pictures as they follow along. Provide ten to fifteen minutes at the end of the session for students to complete a 1–2 page comic identifying the services and materials that are most important to them OR have them create the comic as a library guide for a hypothetical friend who could not participate in the activity.

ADDITIONAL RESOURCES

- View a presentation on this assignment at tinyurl.com/librarystories
- For more ideas and examples of how comics can be used in the library, visit http://tinyurl.com/librarycomics

4. Regional Cuisine: Embedding in the Disciplines

Subject librarians with close ties to their departments report high levels of success with embedded instructional initiatives. With the knowledge that different disciplines have differing expectations for student research, we have gathered a collection of embedded projects from subject librarians working with departments throughout the academy.

Slow-Cooking Method for Librarian Embedding in Chemistry Curriculum Development

Ignacio J. Ferrer-Vinent, Science Research & Instruction Librarian and Associate Professor, University of Colorado Denver, Auraria Library, Denver, Colorado, ignacio.ferrer-vinent@ucdenver.edu

NUTRITION INFORMATION

The librarian's first goal in working on this recipe is to start a library instruction program for organic chemistry at a university where there has never been any information literacy training on the subject. By initiating the program, the librarian would like to introduce the organic chemistry students to library chemistry resources including Sci-Finder and, as time goes on, to develop a collaborative relationship with their chemistry professors. The future end result of this collaboration is to make customized library instruction part of the organic chemistry curriculum. Without the first steps, the end goals can not be reached.

SERVES

Each instruction session serves approximately 20 students in an upper-division chemistry lab, plus the professor.

COOKING TIME

Variable, expect six to seven years. This is not a one class or one semester project. At a university there could be several organic chemistry lab sessions every semester. These sessions are usually taught by different chemistry professors. The librarian wants to convince as many of the professors as possible about the value of having information literacy for their students. Therefore, the time spent on each session throughout the years contributes to the final desired results of library instruction every semester and becoming embedded within the chemistry department.

FIGURE 1. Ingredients for embedded librarianship

INGREDIENTS AND EQUIPMENT

- **Chemistry faculty** who teach the organic chemistry laboratories
- **Lasting relationships** with these professors is paramount in keeping the momentum going towards the end goal—information literacy for all organic chemistry labs. In addition, developing a relationship with a professor who strongly believes in the importance of library instruction for the organic chemistry students will be helpful towards convincing other more reluctant professors. These one or two professors will be your champions within the chemistry department to further your agenda.
- **Library instruction room** equipped with Internet accessible computers for the students to follow during the demonstration and to do related practice. The instructor's computer should be connected to a projection system and to the Internet. Whiteboards are very useful in presenting some of the information, including drawing substances' structural formulas. As an added benefit, being able to move around the room and explain information through different media (i.e. projected screen,

whiteboard, etc.) helps to keep the attention of the students.

- **Access to library chemistry resources** and databases, such as SciFinder.
- **Persistence**. Not all professors will be amenable to allowing the librarian the use of part of the lab time for information literacy. Even if some decline your offer for library instruction, keep them in mind and offer it again the following semester.
- **Patience** is an essential virtue for the librarian to possess in order to be able to persevere and succeed. The librarian should not expect a total acceptance by the chemistry faculty the first time this information literacy opportunity is offered to them.
- **Propriety**. Naturally the librarian will act professionally in all dealings with the faculty. It is important to try to work within the guidelines of the professors and to listen to any of their suggestions.
- **Flexibility**. The librarian can schedule the session rather than requiring the professors to do it through normal channels. Also, the sessions can present as much as possible of what the chemistry professors want shown to their students.

PREPARATION

- About three weeks before the semester begins, the librarian should check the next semester's class schedule to see who teaches organic chemistry labora-

tories. The class schedule also provides contact information of those professors.

- Taking a look at the syllabi for these laboratories (if available) will let you know what is taught in the lab. This information could be useful in communicating with the professors and in planning your information literacy.
- About 10 days before the beginning of the semester the librarian should contact the teaching faculty and offer good, targeted library instruction for their laboratories. Individual emails work well for busy faculty. Be brief in your communication. The email can offer instruction, summarize what the instruction will include, express flexibility, suggest meeting in person, and provide contact information. (See FIGURE 2) Timing is everything. If one is too eager and sends the email more that 10 days prior to the start of the semester, the professors most likely won't be on campus and when they return there would be a flood of emails and your email will be lost. If you wait till the semester is in full swing, the teaching faculty will be too busy to consider your offer and, even if interested, they would not be able to fit it within their plans.
- The librarian should try to become familiar with the resources that are offered so it is possible to deliver on what was promised.
- If a professor responds asking for information literacy, the librarian should

be flexible and helpful in setting up the session. Instead of having the professor schedule the session through the library system, do this for them.

- As time goes on become familiar with these professors—visit with them at the time of individual sessions, be ready to help them if they request something

FIGURE 2. Email to Organic Chemistry Faculty

Sent:	Wednesday, June 12, 2013 3:58 PM
To:	Chemistry.Professor@yu.edu

Hello, *Dr. Organic Chemistry*,

My name is Librarian. I am the Science Instruction Librarian at the *Campus* Library. I would like to propose some library instruction for your students in the Organic Chemistry Laboratory I.

In these library instructions, I usually cover:
- Some key organic chemistry library resources
- How to find journal articles
- Introduction to SciFinder (which takes most of the instruction), covering searches for information on topics, compound information, and synthesis information.

The session usually takes about 1½–2 hours. I am open to your ideas and suggestions. Other types of science references, etc. Please, let me know if you are interested.

Thank you,
Librarian

Librarian Science
Science Instruction Librarian
Campus Library
Your University
123-456-6789
Librarian.Science@yu.edu

of the library, if possible suggest meeting with them before each semester regarding the instruction, etc.

- Keep doing the steps above as needed every semester.

COOKING METHOD

- The librarian teaches library resources for chemistry focusing on SciFinder with in-class practice and time for working on assignments (if any).
  - » The librarian might want to use an online subject guide as an outline or template for the session. This guide can also be helpful to students in the future. A sample LibGuide for Chemistry is available at http://guides.auraria.edu/chemistry. Using the guide, the librarian can show the students some of the specific resources that could be useful to them for the organic chemistry lab.
  - » When demonstrating SciFinder or any other resource, the librarian might consider following the demonstration with some hands-on practice.
  - » If SciFinder is one of the library's databases, the librarian will want to dedicate the majority of the instruction to it. First semester organic chemistry lab students usually need to know how to search for literature and information on substances. For second semester labs, students should learn how to do structure searches and reaction searches in addition to reviewing what they

were shown in the first semester.
  - » In two articles the author discussed his methods for teaching SciFinder to organic chemistry students[1] and exercises used to give practice to the students after aspects of SciFinder are demonstrated.[2]
- The librarian would certainly want to do some pre- and post-assessment of the library session. The assessment will serve as a way to improve the instruction and could also be used as a way to show the chemistry professors how important information literacy is to their organic chemistry students.
- Some of the professors might want to include a short assignment for the students to do during library class. If this is the case, the librarian should understand the nature of that assignment.

Many schools have students purchase lab manuals from academic publishers. However, some universities are beginning to design their own laboratory manuals with experiments more directed to their labs and sold to the students at a more reasonable price. If in time the chance arises, the librarian can offer to contribute by writing a module or chapter for the library instruction day. One item the librarian will want to keep in mind while writing the library module is to keep it short—students will not read a very long piece. This might take two to four weeks to complete and will have to be tried and revised continuously. In the past the author was able to contribute a chapter for a biology lab manual.[3]

ALLERGY WARNINGS

- Do not rush
- Do not be pushy
- Keep in mind that the classes and curriculum are the "property" and responsibility of the chemistry professors.

CHEF'S NOTE

All the time and effort spent is worth it because the students will benefit tremendously and the library would be working as an integral partner in the development of the curriculum. Students as a whole will likely express their satisfaction through open-ended assessment questions. They will find that the instruction facilitates the work they have to do in the laboratory. Later on when the students come to the librarian for assistance, their questions will be more involved. In addition, the chemistry professors will notice improvements on laboratory reports and other assignments. Having library instruction for all the sessions of the organic chemistry lab eliminates the unfair disadvantage of some chemistry students being exposed to these resources while others are not.

NOTES

1. Ignacio J. Ferrer-Vinent, "Teaching SciFinder Basics to Organic Chemistry Students," *Science & Technology Libraries* 31 (2012):164–179.
2. Ignacio J. Ferrer-Vinent, "Using In-class Structured Exercises to Teach SciFinder to Chemistry Students," (forthcoming).
3. Ignacio J. Ferrer-Vinent and Christy A. Carello, "Embedded Library Instruction in a First-Year Biology Laboratory Course," *Science & Technology Libraries* 28 (2008):325–351.

Preparing For Some Sweet Chemistry

Bonnie L. Fong, Rutgers University, bonnie.fong@rutgers.edu

NUTRITION INFORMATION
To teach upper-level undergraduate chemistry majors information literacy skills that will help them successfully complete their course assignments: annotated bibliography, (first draft and final draft of) literature review term paper, poster presentation

COOKING TIME
1 semester

INGREDIENTS AND EQUIPMENT
- Computer classroom
- Chemistry and related science databases (e.g., SciFinder, Web of Science)
- Reference management tool (e.g., RefWorks)
- ACS style guide
- Chemistry writing guides

PREPARATION
Meet with the professor teaching the course to discuss the primary goals of the course. Identify the information literacy skills students need to have in order to fulfill all course requirements. Determine how to best teach them these skills. Find supporting materials and make them available to students—either through their course management system (e.g., Blackboard) or the Reserve Desk. Prepare a LibGuide to complement and supplement their course management system.

COOKING METHOD
Introduce students to general topics such as the difference between original research articles and review articles, what Boolean operators are, how to evaluate information, and how to prevent plagiarism. Demonstrate how to perform efficient and effective searches through the chemical literature using library-subscribed databases (e.g., SciFinder, Web of Science). Allow time for students to perform their own searches and assist them as necessary. Have students follow along when illustrating how to use a reference management tool (e.g., RefWorks). Collect lists of citations from students and provide feedback about their choices.

Provide "sweet" and "sour" writing samples for students to compare. Distinguish between annotated bibliographies and literature reviews. Separate the class into small groups and ask them to discuss what made a sample "sweet" or "sour." Have them share their thoughts for "best practices" with the rest of the class.

Similarly, direct students to various posters put together by scientists and science students. Ask that they consider specific aspects of posters (e.g., font size, layout) as they come up with a list of "best practices" in small groups. Respond to their lists.

Each time after the professor has reviewed student assignments (e.g., annotated bibliographies and drafts of papers), discuss how they turned out. Attend the student poster session and observe how well they present their research.

Evaluate this experience. Determine what the students found most helpful. Assess their assignments to identify where they may still be having trouble. Make tweaks to this recipe for the next time.

ALLERGY WARNINGS
Embedded librarianship in this manner is quite time-consuming—more so if a large class is involved.

CHEF'S NOTE
As a new librarian in a large public research university, this experience offered me the chance to work more closely with one of my liaison areas. I was able to learn more about the information literacy skills—and thus, needs—of students in the chemistry department. I also gained a better understanding of the type of teaching support faculty are interested in. This new perspective has been extremely helpful as I continue to work with other professors in the department. And these opportunities have bloomed, very likely due to positive recommendations from various professors I have worked with in the department. In fact, I expect our collaborations now and into the future will be of some sweet chemistry.

Marinating on Workplace Information Use and Behavior

Chanitra Bishop, Instruction and Emerging Technologies Librarian, Indiana University Bloomington, chbishop@indiana.edu;
Christina Sheley, Head, Business/SPEA Information Commons, Indiana University-Bloomington, cmwilkin@indiana.edu

NUTRITION INFORMATION

This recipe details the use of a blog to embed library and technology instruction, cater to reference needs, and facilitate student marination on workplace information use and behavior.

Business student interns earn a five-star rating from corporate employers when they possess Web 2.0 know-how and advanced information and research skills. Self-reporting from interns indicate gaps in these abilities, realized only once they're "on the job." Two academic librarians and a business faculty whipped up a blog (Information@Work) to communicate with students immersed in the workplace. This recipe also calls for students to reflect on information use and behavior and practicing working in a Web 2.0 environment.

SERVES

Up to 100 students.

COOKING TIME

Semester-long project (recommended minimum: 8 weeks)

INGREDIENTS AND EQUIPMENT

- Blogging software/platform (for this recipe, Wordpress)
- Computer and Internet access

PREPARATION

The librarians set up the blog and send out access notices to students via email. (Note: the blog is set to private to protect any proprietary company information). Next, recruit additional content creators and cook up a pre-determined list of blog posts (optional). Finally, scrape together reflection assignment instructions and grading criteria to serve to students.

COOKING METHOD

Librarians create a welcome post that familiarizes students with the blog's purpose and use and provide assignment parameters, then periodically add posts on information literacy and technology topics (e.g. writing effective blog posts, copyright and blogs, social media and employer practices, and blog and website evaluations, etc.) during cooking time.

Students are required to read all librarian-generated posts and asked to read the welcome post prior to contributing. In addition, they are assigned two, 250-word reflection pieces, requiring description of information use and behavior within a particular company and internship.

Questions to answer include:

- What workplace activities are informed by research and information?
- How is information given to you?
- What types of information sources (books, journals, websites, spreadsheets, raw data, etc.) are you using in your internship?
- What research skills are necessary in your workplace?
- Are there specific information and technology tools you use?

Each reflection assignment is worth 50 points and due the third and ninth week of the course. Librarians read and comment on each reflection entry to provide research guidance and resource suggestions, and full credit is given for completion.

ALLERGY WARNINGS

- Librarians will need to devote significant time in setting up his/her blog, developing assignment parameters, creating content, and interacting with students.
- Students might not read the assignment directions closely, if at all, often requiring the need to explain or redirect.

- Students may not be knowledgeable of blogging software and need guidance on use.

CHEFS' NOTE

The students, librarians, and faculty enjoyed this recipe! The blog made reflection more effective and enjoyable for students. For librarians and faculty, posts and assistance could be adapted quickly and at the point of need. This platform also allowed for seamless integration and the ability to make comments/feedback/suggestions in real time, providing students with individualized service. Librarians gained significant knowledge about information use and behavior in the workplace.

Preparing the Perfect Paper

Claire Clemens, The College of New Jersey, clemensc@tcnj.edu

NUTRITION INFORMATION

This recipe was tested in a class of second-year teacher education students enrolled in a required course on Adolescent Development and Learning. This particular section is a research practicum intended to promote undergraduate research at the college. After several semesters of standard one-shot instruction, the class professor and the librarian collaborated over the summer to identify the specific information literacy skills needed to become researchers in the field of teacher education. This project works best with 10–15 students

COOKING TIME

Three class sessions in the library over the course of a semester.

ACRL INFORMATION DIETARY STANDARDS ADDRESSED

Information Literacy Standards for Teacher Education (http://www.ala.org/acrl/sites/ala.org.acrl/files/content/standards/ilstandards_te.pdf)

INGREDIENTS AND EQUIPMENT

Library classroom with tables for small groups and computer stations for each student

PREPARATION

- Collaborate with teaching professor
- Find lots of good examples
- Develop rubrics

COOKING METHOD
Session 1

Standard One. The information literate teacher education student defines and articulates the need for information and selects strategies and tools to find that information.

LESSON 1: Understanding the assignment; determining the scope of the research need; defining a topic; and identifying key concepts

1. The librarian outlines the nature of the final research product and the due date.
   - » *1.A.2. Factors that influence the information need (nature extent, type, format, intended audience)*
2. Discuss how research topics fit into the overall course objectives.
3. The librarian assigns a broad topic area to each student.
   - » *1.A.4. Defining or modifying the information need to a more manageable focus.*
4. The librarian introduces general information resources, specifically books and reference books and allows time for students to explore books. Selected articles marked for quick access.
   - » *1.A.3 Exploring general information sources to increase familiarity with the scope of the need.*

- » *1.B.2. Breaking down information need into component concepts and terms.*
5. The librarian introduces search strategies for the library catalog, including the varying uses of keywords and formal subject terms. Students then spend time searching the library catalog.
   - » *1.B.3. Brainstorming and selecting synonyms and alternative words that represent the component concepts.*

RESEARCH ASSIGNMENT #1: Write a one-paragraph overview of your topic, a list of relevant search terms (see sample), and a reference list containing a minimum of three book resources. You will turn in 4 pages, using APA formatting as outlined below. Please see rubric for grading details.

Session 2

Standard Two. The information literate teacher education student locates and selects information based on its appropriateness to the specific information need (and the developmental needs of the student).

LESSON 2: Understanding the nature of academic research and how information is produced, organized, and accessed. Locating and selecting information.

1. The librarian introduces the Information Literacy Standards for Teacher Education and review the research skills covered in Lesson 1 and reflects on Assignment 1.
2. Students construct a definition of three types of periodicals by sorting issues of popular magazines, trade publications, and scholarly journals into three piles. Characteristics of each type are identified and discussed.
   » *1.C.2. Outcome: Understanding how information in the discipline of education and related behavioral and social sciences is formally and informally produced, organized, disseminated, described, accessed and preserved.*
3. Students examine a scholarly article to understand the elements of scholarly research and how it is a primary source vs. a secondary source.
   » *1.C.4. Outcome: Recognizing that fulfilling the information need may require combining existing information with original thought, experimentation, and/or analysis to produce new information.*
4. The librarian demonstrates techniques and strategies for database searching, including how to access research databases and how to most efficiently and effectively search ERIC. The librarian reinforces the concept of keyword vs. subject term searching.
   » *1.D.1 Outcome: Knowing where the needed information of the desired types and formats is available and how it can be accessed.*

5. Students practice search strategies in ERIC with the goal of finding one or more articles on their own topics.
   » *2.A.3. Outcome: Choosing and utilizing efficient and effective approaches for locating information in the selected tools.*
   » *2.B.3. Outcome: Choosing the relevant content from a source to meet the information need.*
6. Explanation of Research Assignment 2. What is an annotated bibliography? Hand out assignment description, example, and rubric.

RESEARCH ASSIGNMENT #2:
PART 1: Identify three scholarly articles on your topic from a minimum of three different journals. Write an annotated bibliography using APA Style.

PART 2: Find ten scholarly articles relevant to your topic. Bring paper copies of all ten scholarly articles to the next library session. (This may include the three articles used for the annotated bibliography.)

Session 3
Standard Three. The information literate teacher education student organizes and analyzes the information in the context of specific information needs and the developmental appropriateness for the audience.

Standard Six. The information literate teacher education student knows how to ethically use and disseminate information.

LESSON 3: Writing in stages (Introduction to Paper, Annotated Bibliography, Literature Review), Citing Sources, Paraphrasing vs. Quotations

1. ACTIVITY: Each student sorts the 10 research articles due for class into three piles by major themes. Each student describes to the class how his/her paper outline is based on the overall topic and themes from the literature review.
   » *3.A.1. Outcome: Using various processes to maintain, organize, and manage located resources.*
   » *3.B.1. Outcome: Analyzing the structure, logic, and presentation of information and any supporting arguments or methods.*
   » *3.B.5. Outcome: Recognizing the usefulness of and differences between information sources.*
2. The significance of citing sources.
   » *6.1. Understanding the ethical, legal, and socio-economic issues surrounding information and information technology.*
3. Students correct one another's APA citations on the annotated bibliography from Assignment 2.
   » *6.5. Selecting and using an appropriate documentation style to cite or give credit to original information sources.*
4. The librarian presents the three forms of In-text citations—(Short Quote, Long Quote, Paraphrasing) HANDOUT

5. ACTIVITY: Look at the 10 articles brought to class—find examples of each of the three types of in-text citations. Match the in-text citation to the full-citation in the reference list. Next, choose a quote from one of your own articles and determine how to correctly cite it in-text.

6. Presentation on how to paraphrase YouTube video How to Use APA In-Text Citations to Avoid Plagiarism http://www.youtube.com/watch?v=2644z1Nf6Tc Examples provided on HANDOUT

7. Students complete a paraphrasing activity, using a passage provided by the librarian.
    »   *6.4. Demonstrating an understanding of what constitutes plagiarism; Giving proper credit to others' ideas.*

ALLERGY WARNINGS
Collaboration with teaching professor must work well. Due dates must mesh with other class assignments.

CHEF'S NOTE
The students continued to write in stages. During the final library session, the class professor spoke to the students about turning in a 3-page introduction to the paper together with a reference list of all the books and articles they had selected. This was done to have them to begin in-text citing correctly based on the reference list. Assembling the paper in this way meant students devoted more time to perfecting each section.

The professor reported student papers received higher grades than in previous semesters as the students followed directions more closely. Students asked the librarian more frequently for assistance outside of class. Librarian was able to establish a rapport with students, not normally possible in one-shot instruction.

ADDITIONAL RESOURCES
*   Online tutorials
*   YouTube video
*   Handouts
*   LibGuide on Adolescent Development & Learning http://libguides.tcnj.edu/adolescent

Embedded Librarian for a Writing Course in the Clinical Nurse Leader Program

Lin Wu, MLIS, AHIP, Health Sciences Librarian and Associate Professor, University of Tennessee Health Science Center Library, Memphis, TN, lwu5@uthsc.edu

NUTRITION INFORMATION

The goal of the embedded librarian pilot project is to improve the student experience, outcomes, and information literacy skills for researching and writing. A health sciences librarian was integrated into a 2-credit intensive writing course in the Clinical Nurse Leader (CNL) Program for the College of Nursing.

SERVES

70+ students

COOKING TIME

One semester

INGREDIENTS AND EQUIPMENT

- *The Publication Manual of the American Psychological Association* (APA), 6th edition
- Scholarly writing
- EndNote 6 program
- One-on-one research consultations
- Pre- and post-surveys for program evaluation
- Digital instructional material or tutorial creation using technologies (e.g., screencasts and videos)

PREPARATION

- Be willing to accept and challenge change
- Communicate effectively with the course faculty
- Review course syllabus
- Review course required reading materials
- Identify librarian embedded content/role for the course
- Understand course assignment rubrics or grading criteria
- Familiar with writing and formatting rules of the APA 6th edition
- Familiar with using Blackboard, the course management system (CMS)
- Familiar with EndNote program for scholarly writing

COOKING METHOD

- Communication skills
- Collaboration skills
- Librarian-instructor and partner skills
- Scholarly writing skills
- Skills in applying technologies to create digital library resources such as creating a course research guide using LibGuides, the most widely used system for creating research guides and sharing knowledge
- A presentation in using APA 6th edition for course assignments targeting student commonly made APA errors.
- A FAQ session to address individual student's APA questions
- One-on-one research consultations virtually and face-to-face to review student papers and their citations and references for their papers

ALLERGY WARNINGS

- Students have difficulty following APA 6th edition rules to cite and reference their course assignments.
- There might be gaps between course faculty expectation and student performance.

CHEF'S NOTE

An embedded librarian is not a regular librarian. They are partners and team members for the course they are embedded. Librarians embedded into courses with intensive research and writing components need strong time commitment to provide at the point of need assistance for students. The key to ensure the program success is for the librarian to understand the course content, course outcome, and course faculty expectations of the student achievement.

PICO de Gallo:
Spicing Up Evidence-Based Nursing Research

Cass Kvenild, Head, Learning Resource Center, University of Wyoming Libraries, ckvenild@uwyo.edu; Jenny Garcia, Health Sciences Librarian, University of Wyoming Libraries, jgarcia@uwyo.edu

NUTRITION INFORMATION

University of Wyoming nursing students are required to formulate clinical research questions using the PICO(T) process. The PICO(T) model of posing a question ensures that approaches to the literature review follow evidence-based practice guidelines.

Students will each formulate a PICO(T) question using the following template:
P: Patient, Population, or Problem
I: Intervention
C: Comparison
O: Outcome
(T: Time)

In (P)_____ how does

(I)_____ compared to (C)__

affect (O)_____?

For example: "In surgical patients (P), does pneumatic intermittent compression devices (I), compared to compression stockings (C), reduce the incidence of deep vein thrombosis(O)?"

SERVES

Up to 3 classes of 30 online nursing students

COOKING TIME

Four intensive, hands-on weeks

INGREDIENTS AND EQUIPMENT

- Two librarians
- Access to course management system
- Evidence-based practice (EBP) resources and database(s) of systematic reviews
- Dedicated time to review research questions and guide search strategies

PREPARATION

Prior to the semester start, librarians meet with nursing instructors to review the course timeline and assignment expectations. Librarians should review evidence-based research guidelines, practice formulating questions using the PICO(T) format, and review nursing and health databases to determine library holdings and any new resources.

For the purposes of this assignment, librarians and students will utilize the definition of evidence-based practice developed by nursing professors Nola A. Schmidt and Janet M. Brown "EBP is a process involving the examination and application of research findings or other reliable evidence that has been integrated with scientific theories.

For nurses to participate in this process, they must use their critical thinking skills to review research publications and other sources of information. After the information is evaluated, nurses use their clinical decision-making skills to apply evidence to patient care. As in all nursing care, patient preferences and needs are the basis of care decisions and therefore essential to EBP."

COOKING METHOD

Introduce two embedded librarians to the online course management system (CMS) during four separate weeks in the semester to provide an introduction to library resources for evidence-based practice and to provide one-on-one feedback in the construction of PICO(T) questions and related search techniques.

THE EMBEDDED PROJECT

Weeks 1 and 2: The instructor will introduce students to the PICO(T) method of asking research questions. The students will describe a scenario that might result in a nursing decision could result in a change of practice.

Students will post their PICO(T) questions in the course management system discussion boards, where librarians and the instructor will review the questions and provide feedback on how they can be improved. Every element of the PICO(T) question might need to be revised or re-worded, especially when students are new to the process, so it is good to have the eyes of the instructor and both librarians on this section of the course. Once the PICO(T) questions have been approved by the instructor, students begin the literature search.

Week 3: Librarians provide an introduction to online library resources within the course management system via short videos and online guides. Emphasis should be on specialized resources required for evidence-based nursing research (such as the Cochrane Library or Joanna Briggs Institute), as well as general nursing literature sources (like PubMed and CINAHL). Instructor will provide reminders of how to read scientific articles, with specialized instruction on reading the literature of evidence-based practice.

Week 4: Students will share their search strategies and sources in the discussion boards, where librarians will offer feedback on search strategies and on selecting and using evidence-based sources. In some cases, this will be a review of the content offered in Week 3. In other cases, the PICO(T) questions may require extended re-tooling and revised search strategies.

Guided by the "tiers of evidence" model, students are expected to find the best

evidence available and evaluate it. Librarians should be prepared to guide students through searching systematic reviews (such as the Cochrane Library) and finding quantitative studies within PubMed or CINAHL. It has been documented that a low comfort level with advanced search techniques and challenges with critically appraising research are two major barriers to implementing evidence-based practice. Librarians are a crucial resource at this step in the learning process.

ALLERGY WARNINGS

Be prepared for lots of questions from nursing students who are new to evidence-based practice and who may not be expert searchers. The PICO(T) concept is not intuitive for all students, and the first drafts of questions almost always require revisions. Expect that some students may develop beautifully written questions, which are not searchable, due to lack of studies on the chosen intervention. Some students may

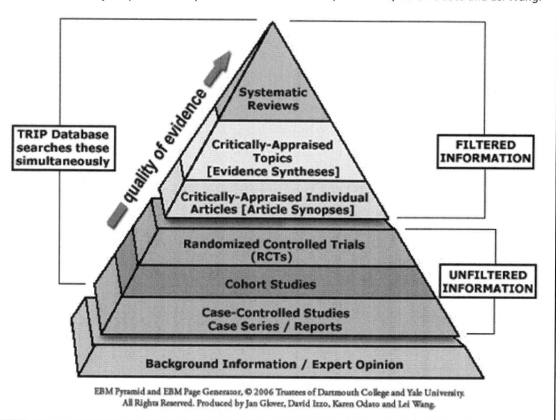

FIGURE 1. The Evidence-based Medicine Pyramid, Copyright 2006–2011. Trustees of Dartmouth College and Yale University. Re-printed with permission from Jan Glover, David Izzo, Karen Odato and Lei Wang.

have severe reactions to subject headings (MeSH Terms) and filters/limiters, after years of exposure to Google-like searches.

While this recipe can be completed by one librarian instead of two, the solo librarian will need to have both subject expertise and a great deal of time available. We strongly recommend incorporating two librarians if possible. In our case, one librarian possessed significant expertise in searching the nursing literature, while the other brought comfort and experience with online guides, videos, and course management systems. Both librarians attended specialized trainings on evidence-based practice and on PICO(T) questions prior to embedding in the course, including those offered by the Medical Library Association, regional medical library associations, and the College of Nursing.

CHEFS' NOTE
This assignment forms close bonds between nursing instructors, students, and librarians. Expect to hear from the students and teachers for years after this assignment as they continue to refine their search strategies while utilizing evidence-based practice approaches in their clinical practice.

ADDITIONAL RESOURCES
- *The Cochrane Library*. http://www.thecochranelibrary.com/
- Garcia, Jenny. *PICO Questions: a tutorial*. http://libguides.uwyo.edu/PICOT-tutorial

- Garcia, Jenny and Conerton, Kate. *BSN Students' Guide to Evidence-based Practice* http://libguides.uwyo.edu/EBP-BSN
- The Joanna Briggs Institute. http://joannabriggs.org/
- Schmidt, Nola A. and Brown, Janet M. *Evidence-Based Practice for Nurses: Appraisal and Application of Research*. Sudbury: Jones & Bartlett Learning, 2012.

Five-Course Meal Infused with Information Skills and Resources

Kimberly Whalen, Health Science Librarian and Assistant Professor of Library Services, Valparaiso University, kimberly.whalen@valpo.edu; Suzanne Zentz, Assistant Professor of Nursing, Valparaiso University, suzanne.zentz@valpo.edu

NUTRITION INFORMATION

This hearty menu blends a librarian throughout an on-campus undergraduate nursing research course.

SERVES

Serves an undergraduate nursing research class with up to 80 students

COOKING TIME

This five-course meal spans one semester. To develop flavors properly, simmer, taste, and adjust seasoning as necessary.

American Association of Colleges of Nursing Essentials of Baccalaureate Education for Professional Nursing Practice Standards Addressed

Essential Three: 3.2, 3.4, 3.5, 3.7
Essential Four: 1.1

INGREDIENTS AND EQUIPMENT

- Nursing professor and librarian collaboration
- Regular librarian class attendance
- Librarian time dedicated to grading assignments outside of class
- Course textbook for librarian
- Access to course management system
- Computer lab with instructor station and computer for each student
- Access to article databases and Internet resources
- Materials to create:
  - » PowerPoints with voice narration of lecture
  - » Handout of search tips and suggested resources
  - » Handout showing first pages of primary research and non-primary research articles (literature review or opinion article)
  - » Blank Individual Research Log Worksheet (figure 1.)
  - » Handout depicting levels of evidence
  - » Sample of evidence summary, best practice information sheet, systematic review, clinical practice guideline, and primary research article
  - » Handout explaining MeSH and CINAHL subject headings, samples of sophisticated searches, and advanced search tips

PREPARATION

1. Nursing professor and librarian
   - Discuss course learning objectives, assignments, grading rubrics, and expectations of involvement in class sessions.
   - Develop class schedule that integrates librarian and information resources relative to assignment due dates.
   - Integrate research logs within course assignments. (Research logs document search conducted, critical appraisal of information utilized, and reflection on difficulties and lessons learned).
2. Nursing professor creates PowerPoint with voice narration of lecture material to free up class time for information content.
3. Librarian
   - Discusses time commitment with library colleagues and administration prior to committing.
   - Gains access to a laptop or tablet for each class session so technology is readily available to support impromptu reference and research questions.
4. Nursing professor
   - Lists librarian name and contact information on course syllabi.
   - Provides librarian access to class within course management system.
5. Librarian creates class and assignment-specific resource guide using Spring-Share LibGuides or other system. Links

guide to course within course management system.

COOKING METHOD
First Course: Hors D'oeuvres
1. Nursing professor
   - Introduces librarian at first and second class sessions.
2. Librarian
   - Explains role in course and provide in-person and online contact information.
   - Following in-person introduction, posts welcome message to class within course management system.

Second Course: Soup
1. Prior to the first hands-on information session, have students read a chapter in their text and watch a 20 minute PowerPoint with voice narration describing how to search for nursing information.
2. Make plans to hold class session in a computer classroom within the library.
3. Nursing professor
   - Discusses first assignment which requires students to locate a primary research article. Provides students topic ideas including pain management in the elderly or reality shock among newly graduated nurses.
   - Reinforces importance of using library provided databases to find quality information for course assignments.
4. Librarian
   - Discusses differences between

primary and secondary sources of information.
   - Distributes handout showing the first pages of a primary research and a non-primary research article. Ask students to locate clues which identify the type of article under review.

- Discusses importance of developing a systematic search for information.
- Demonstrates how to document search process, resources searched, and results.
- Distributes individual research log worksheet.

FIGURE 1. Individual Research Log Worksheet

What is your topic? _____

What keywords or phrases do you hope will be in the "perfect" research article on your topic?
_____ , _____ , _____

Jot down other terms (synonyms) that could be used for the keywords or phrases above.
_____ OR _____ OR _____

Now jot down the best information resources/databases for your research.
_____ , _____ , _____

After you've thought about your topic, keywords/search terms, and databases, log in and search. Which database/resource did you use to find your primary research article? _____

How many articles (results) were yielded from your best/final search? _____

What keywords/phrases were used in the search strategy that located your research article?
_____ , _____ , _____

Did you end up using CINAHL Headings or MeSH in your search?
_____ , _____ , _____

What limiters did you use in the search that located your research article? (Date range, language, or any other limiting criteria used)
_____ , _____ , _____

Why did you select that specific primary research article? How did it match your topic of interest? How did it meet the needs of this assignment? How current was the research? Were the findings significant?

_____

What difficulties did you have locating an appropriate primary research article for this assignment?

_____

The next time you use a scholarly database to search for evidence, what will you do differently?

_____

- In large group, brainstorms potential keywords, synonyms, and subject headings related to librarian example.
- Have students fill in individual research log worksheets for their chosen topic. Have students document keywords and synonyms that can be used to find information.

5. Librarian
   - Distributes handout of search tips and suggested resources.
   - Demonstrates searches for primary research articles within CINAHL and MEDLINE databases.
   - Demonstrates Boolean operators, combining terms, subject headings, and other appropriate limiters.
6. Have students conduct a search for information, document search structure and results on research log worksheet.
7. Librarian and nursing professor assist with questions during allotted hands-on time.
8. Librarian grades student research logs using rubrics developed collaboratively with nursing professor.
9. Nursing professor grades rest of assignment using rubrics discussed with librarian.

THROUGHOUT THE MEAL

1. Librarian
   - Brings textbook, course lecture notes, and relevant handouts to each class session.
   - Participates, as appropriate, in discussions during each class session.

- Posts announcements, as appropriate, highlighting search tips or resource suggestions within course management system.
2. Nursing professor
   - Involves the librarian, as appropriate, in information related questions during class sessions and in-class activities.

Third Course: Salad

1. Prior to this class session, students read a chapter in their text about levels of evidence.
2. Session takes place in regular classroom.
3. Librarian
   - Leads discussion about levels of evidence related to nursing practice.
   - Provides handout depicting the levels of evidence used in course textbook.
   - Distributes an evidence summary, best practice information sheet, systematic review, clinical practice guideline, and primary study all related to same clinical question. Discusses each type of evidence in detail.
   - Explains to students how primary research articles lead to secondary analysis and higher levels of evidence.
   - Demonstrates searches for secondary information sources within Joanna Briggs Institute Evidence Database, The Cochrane Library, and National Guideline Clearinghouse.

- Asks for student volunteers to assist with demonstrations.

Fourth Course: Entree

1. Session takes place in regular classroom.
2. Nursing professor
   - Discusses second assignment, which is a group project involving searching for the best evidence to address a nursing clinical question. Clinical questions could include identifying the best screening tool for depression or the best practices for fasting prior to surgery.
   - Places students into randomly assigned groups.
   - Discusses best practices for conducting a systematic group search versus an individual search.
3. Librarian
   - Reinforces the systematic search process by demonstrating a sophisticated database search using multiple keywords, at least one subject heading, and multiple limiters. Discusses why groups should begin their search for information in secondary sources of information like the Cochrane Library instead of within a predominantly primary source of information like CINAHL.
   - Provides handout explaining MeSH and CINAHL subject headings, samples of sophisticated searches, and advanced search tips.
4. Nursing professor distributes clinical scenarios to groups. Provides groups time

to read the assignment, ask questions about their clinical scenario, and begin their work.

5. Librarian and nursing professor move around room and assist with questions.

THROUGHOUT THE MEAL

1. Librarian and nursing professor
   - Answer student questions through one-on-one and group meetings outside of class sessions.
   - Answer student questions via email and telephone.

Fifth Course: Dessert

1. Session takes place in computer classroom within library.
2. Have students sit in assigned groups.
3. Librarian
   - Discusses importance of developing a systematic search for information.
   - Demonstrates how to document search process, resources searched, and results.
   - Distributes group research log worksheet.
4. Student groups
   - Brainstorm potential keywords, synonyms, and subject headings related to assigned clinical question.
   - Document concepts on group research log worksheet.
   - Conduct a search for information using group developed strategies.
   - Document search structures and results on group research log worksheet.

5. Librarian and nursing professor move around the room and assist with questions.
6. Librarian grades completed group research logs using rubrics developed collaboratively with nursing professor.
7. Nursing professor grades rest of assignment using rubrics discussed with librarian.

ALLERGY WARNINGS

Embedding within an on-campus course can be time consuming. Work with subject professor to strategically identify class times with best chances for interaction. At minimum try to attend at least ½ of class time each week.

Students might be confused as to the role of the librarian both within and outside of class sessions. Make sure introduction at start of semester is clear. Reiterate roles and responsibilities throughout semester.

Undergraduate students are often over confident of their information searching skills. Some initial resistance to building these skills is to be expected. Involving students in hands-on activities can highlight skills that need improvement as well as create active learning opportunities.

CHEFS' NOTE

- It is important to plan librarian led discussions around assignment deadlines.
- Be strategic about where the librarian led sessions take place—instruction both within the nursing classroom and

the library reinforces librarian integration.
- Librarian attendance at class related events such as group poster presentations further enhances the relationship with students.
- Using nursing professor developed PowerPoint with voice narrations outside of class frees up class time for active learning.
- Incorporating time for hands-on searching, group project work, and interaction with nursing professor and librarian positively impacts student learning outcomes.
- Consider embedding in a course early on in a curriculum so students will get to know "their librarian" before enrolling in more research intensive courses.
- Research log worksheets are a big hit with students. The worksheets act as a step-by-step guide through the information search process.

Preparing Online Doctoral Students for Success

Swapna Kumar, University of Florida, swapnakumar@coe.ufl.edu; Marilyn Ochoa, Associate Library Director, SUNY-Oswego, marilyn.ochoa@oswego.edu

NUTRITION INFORMATION

The College of Education at the University of Florida began a professional practice doctorate in Educational Technology in 2008. Activities and research in the program require students to integrate peer-reviewed literature into their writing, craft annotated bibliographies, and review prior research before they conduct their own. Students' ability to access, find, evaluate, and synthesize prior research contributes largely to their progress in the doctoral program and their development as scholar-practitioners. Incoming online students are working professionals, several of who are returning to academic pursuits after a break. They are not all aware of digital resources and scholarship in the field of educational technology and are not familiar with the use of online library databases. The importance of information literacy support was highlighted during research conducted with the first group of students in the online doctoral program where one-third of students reported that increased library instruction was needed for student success in the doctoral program. The education librarian and educational technology program coordinator thus collaborated to pilot a program-integrated embedded librarian project during the first year of the program for a second group of doctoral students.

SERVES

Incoming students to the online doctoral program in educational technology come from various disciplines such as mathematics, science, art, instructional design, or nursing, and work in diverse environments (e.g., elementary education, middle or high school, higher education, military). The group of incoming students in the first project numbered 23.

COOKING TIME

One year, revised and being repeated with the next group of students two years later.

INGREDIENTS AND EQUIPMENT

- Online survey software
- Screencasting software
- Course management system access
- Headphone and microphone
- LibGuide developed for easy access to education related resources
- Video tutorials on essential information literacy topics: identifying and accessing databases from off campus, developing effective search strategies, writing annotated bibliographies and using bibliographic management systems
- Ask the Librarian Discussion forum

PREPARATION

1. Review the literature. In an attempt to design the best possible information literacy instruction for the online program, first prior research on library instruction for online students was reviewed. Valuable lessons could be learned from the literature on the types of instruction provided to online learners (synchronous and asynchronous formats) and duration (embedded, course-integrated, or one-shot).

2. Identify crucial information literacy skills. Based on a review of doctoral program expectations, the librarian compiled a list of crucial information literacy skills that would help online students succeed.

3. Target specific assignments. For our specific context we decided that program-integrated instruction that targeted specific assignments (e.g. searching for dissertations, finding peer-reviewed research, writing an annotated bibliography) in the first year of the program was important.

4. Conduct a needs analysis. Considering the wide range of skills and backgrounds of incoming online doctoral students in the educational technology program, we conducted a needs assessment of online students' prior knowledge and skills before they began the program. This included students' perceived ability to use resources, find appropriate literature, cite and evaluate resources, and their preference of library

instruction formats. Students' survey responses (n = 21; 91%) were combined with the information literacy content identified by the librarian to design the content and format of the embedded librarian interactions.

5. Develop standard tutorials and customized just-in-time resources. Based on Kimok and Heller-Ross' conclusion that it is important to not only provide pre-created standard tutorials in a course, but to also create such tutorials in response to student needs during a course, we decided that in the online doctoral program, essential information literacy topics identified by the education librarian would first be addressed in pre-created tutorials. Later, online students' needs would be surveyed both at the beginning and during the year to create asynchronous resources that they could use.

COOKING METHOD

Librarian embedded in the first year, from orientation session through fall, spring and summer semester provided instruction in both asynchronous and synchronous formats. Content in the first semester included accessing resources from off-campus, the different databases important to education, identifying peer-reviewed resources, and citing in APA style. Later content included using Refworks and writing annotated bibliographies.

ALLERGY WARNINGS

- Don't rely solely on students' self-reports of information literacy skills and self-efficacy. A needs analysis survey is important but it is also important for the librarian and program faculty to identify requisite information literacy skills that all students should possess.
- Don't rely completely on students' professed preference for one format of instruction over the other, but provide as many forms of interaction with the librarian as possible. Students might not be aware of certain formats or instructional possibilities.
- Don't assume students will interact with the instruction provided by the librarian. Mandate the viewing of asynchronous content and attendance of synchronous sessions that is crucial to students' information literacy and success in the program and to assess students' learning of the content with simple tasks.

CHEFS' NOTE

A needs assessment was very important because working professionals returning to a graduate program have varying levels of abilities and familiarity with university resources. However, the identification of information literacy topics that are crucial to doctoral student success that was collaboratively identified by the librarian and program coordinator was more important, because students often 'did not know what they did not know.'

Continuous assessment of how the embedded librarian interactions and instruction is working and the evolving need of students as they progress through the online program was invaluable: to adapt the content and format of instruction; to assess the usefulness and success of the embedded librarian; to develop new instruction in addition to the pre-created online instructional resources; and to determine which students need more support than others.

Providing embedded librarian interactions using different media and multiple formats of instruction was useful because some students appreciate the real-time interaction with the librarian and others prefer step-by-step asynchronous resources such as tutorials or PDFs. We could have sent out more messages or resources to students at regular intervals so that they were reminded that the librarian was present in the course or program and available to help. We found that students accessed embedded librarian resources or interactions at strategic times during the course or program, e.g. when assignments are due. For the next group, the asynchronous resources were placed at strategic points where students are reminded that they are available, e.g. next to assignments or content in the course.

Faculty-librarian collaboration was essential and contributed to our success at every step of the process: From the identification of student needs and resources to the publication of assessment results of the project, the continuous collaboration between faculty and academic librarians was important to the integration of information literacy instruction at every point in the online program.

Tantalizing Treats:
Scholarly Research in Sensitive Subjects

*Beth E. Tumbleson, Assistant Director, Gardner-Harvey Library, Miami University Middletown, tumbleb@miamioh.edu;
Collaborating with Richelle Frabotta, M.S.Ed., AASECT Certified Sexuality Educator, frabotrr@miamioh.edu*

NUTRITION INFORMATION

Teaching undergraduates information literacy skills related to human sexuality in family studies and social work or sociology requires the right mix of scholarly research strategies and approachability on the learning management system (LMS) embedded librarian's part.

SERVES

This recipe feeds from 30–175 students in traditional, hybrid, or online courses which rely on the LMS and involve faculty-librarian collaboration.

The goals of the recipe are:

1. To develop online academic research skills in undergraduates enrolled in family life sexuality education courses, requiring research papers and presentations on professionals within the field or thematic topics within the discipline.
2. To expand awareness of the many subject-specific databases and finding tools available through university library collections, previously unknown to many students, who rely heavily on a few, familiar, free Internet sources.
3. To motivate students to apply critical thinking, creative problem-solving, and perseverance in searching for real-world

biographical information and accurate, academic information on human sexuality issues globally.

4. To encourage librarian-student interaction in online research consultations where students may understandably be reluctant to seek guidance.

COOKING TIME

One semester or quarter.

INGREDIENTS AND EQUIPMENT

- Faculty-librarian collaboration
- Access to the LMS
- Subject-specific databases and eBooks
- Citation generators
- Digital tutorials
- Search strategies
- Picture and contact information
- Willingness to engage students proactively and respectfully
- Reflective worksheet (optional)

PREPARATION

1. Discuss learning outcomes with the instructor for the research component of the course.
2. Discover the research challenges students encounter from the professor's perspective.

3. Recommended: read the course-required book to get a flavor for what students will be learning and pondering.
4. Compile a list of relevant library databases, eBook reference titles, evaluation tutorials, and finding tools.
5. Design a research worksheet for students to reflect on the research process, the search terms used, databases searched, and strategies employed to revise a search that yields insufficient information.
6. See Figure 1 (next page)
7. Post library resources either on the embedded librarian page in the LMS course or by the research assignment.

COOKING METHOD

1. Use the mail tool to introduce yourself and your role to students, library resources and services available, and contact information so that students may email/IM/text/call you with individual questions when need arises.
2. Follow-up at intervals with additional research strategies and links to library databases as needed as you become aware of areas where one student is stuck or struggling, so all may benefit.
3. In all-student communications, keep the tone encouraging, language clear, the message practical, and resources easy to

FIGURE 1. Mapping the Research Process: The Sexy Road to Scholarship

Conducting scholarly research takes thought and time. Be prepared to adopt new research strategies and resources as you search online, especially in a field that is new to you and one that is as provocative as sexuality education.

Name: _____
Sexuality professional (Full name):

Research topic (Narrowed, brief overview of your focus area):

Research question:
(Write your topic as a single research question which will drive your research as you try to answer it.)

List the research databases you searched to find scholarly journal articles, newspaper articles, online encyclopedia and dictionary overview essays, etc.

List the keywords and subject terms you used in searching research databases and online catalogs. (At least 3)

List the search engines you used. (Examples include: Google.com/Scholar.google.com/Ask.com)

Write out the EXACT "search string" or "search query" you entered in that mysterious search box for Google or other search engine.

Name a research strategy/source, you learned about or you further developed in connection with this project.

Describe one **research or information problem you encountered** in connection with this research assignment and **how you solved** it. (At least 1 paragraph)

- Be mindful of the discomfort students may be experiencing with the topic of human sexuality as well as with academic research. Maintain a positive, professional, and patient interaction style.
- Streamline scholarly research somewhat so that students get started with the best databases and reference eBooks available through the university library.
- Remember trusted relationships in research are built over time. Give yourself grace as you work as an LMS embedded librarian.

CHEFS' NOTE

If presented with the opportunity to read the research worksheets students submit, do so. You will learn much. Summarize your discoveries through the lens of an academic librarian. Take these findings into consideration as you guide students in future semesters. Share findings with the faculty member. Do not be surprised if you are invited to share these insights with students next semester.

ADDITIONAL RESOURCES

- Kristof, N. D., & WuDunn, S. (2009). *Half the Sky: Turning Oppression into Opportunity for Women Worldwide*. New York: Alfred A. Knopf.
- LexisNexis: Finding Foreign Newspapers (2 minute screencast; produced by Beth Tumbleson; 2013) http://screencast-o-matic.com/watch/clnIYAVIDE
- LexisNexis: International News Stories (2 minute screencast; produced by Beth Tumbleson; 2013) http://screencast-o-matic.com/watch/clnXYzVl8P

access. Use catchy email subject lines, for example: "When library databases let you down."

4. Acknowledge the frustrating challenges all researchers face, the time and effort required, and the necessity of using resources and tools (which may be unfamiliar but are employed by those working in the field).

5. Include the instructor in the communication circle, so she may learn how students respond to research obstacles and share subject expertise and professional insights with student(s).

6. Build trusted student-librarian relationships by working out of a mindset of warmth, empathy, and respect.

ALLERGY WARNINGS

- In consulting students chiefly through email, be aware of its limitations. Misunderstandings happen more readily in this format vs. face-to-face reference interviews.

Cooking up a Concept Map with Prezi:
Conceptualizing the Artist Statement

Katie Greer, First-Year Experience and Art Liaison Librarian, Oakland University, Rochester, Michigan, greer@oakland.edu

NUTRITION INFORMATION

Studio art students do not typically have many formal research projects, and thus the process of research when it comes time to write their artist statements can be very overwhelming, leading to poorly articulated theses and artist statements, or bibliographies that make professors wince. This session aims to introduce them to one of the first steps in the research process: generating keywords and themes to explore with further research. This project provides two main results, the first of which is an important introduction for studio art students to the beginning research process, conceptualizing their own artistic objectives, and thinking about their place within the art historical canon. Second, it serves as an important contact point for the librarian to provide feedback on relevant resources and research topics for each student.

Prezi, although normally a presentation tool, lends itself very well to a project of this nature due to its ease of use and its aesthetics. Students who have never used it before can quickly familiarize themselves with its basic functions, and the setup allows for more creative expression in drawing out concept maps than in more traditional concept mapping software, including seemingly unlimited space and the ability to easily paste images and video content onto the map.

SERVES

Due to the time needed for the grading/feedback portion of this assignment, no more than 20 students is recommended.

COOKING TIME

Roughly 45 minutes of instruction time, plus variable time allowed as needed for students to work on their assignments in-class. This session is most useful when combined with an additional session on the tools of research available from the library. What resources should students use with their newly generated research ideas? What are the best practices for using those resources?

INGREDIENTS AND EQUIPMENT

- Computer access for all students
- Instructor's station and projection or screen control option
- Prezi account

COOKING METHOD

This session takes place in a computer lab or a classroom in which students have access to laptops, so that they may have time to work on their concept maps with the librarian there. It could also easily be adapted for the online environment.

PREPARATION

Before the session, the librarian prepares a sample concept map using Prezi that explores either a single theme or uses an image as a starting point for keyword/idea generation. A list of further concept mapping resources is created, either via a handout or course website, as well as guidelines for the concept mapping assignment.

THE EMBEDDED PROJECT

1. The librarian explains the purpose of the activity: to think conceptually about research and to communicate their artistic objectives to others. What questions are they exploring? What themes inspire them or do they want to explore further?

2. The librarian introduces concept mapping by showing the sample Prezi and encouraging the students to start with either a single idea/word, a question, or an inspirational image. The librarian facilitates discussion of the sample prezi. This example might include free association keywords with the topic, or include a set of formal questions to help draw out the content, such as "How?,"

"What?," "Where?" "Who?," "When?," etc. The example should illustrate the inclusion of visual examples—both canonical artists' work related to the theme and a selection of images by the concept map creator to illustrate how an artist may start thinking about themes in his or her own work.

3. After the technique of concept mapping has been covered, the librarian creates a blank Prezi and starts a thematic concept map with class input. As ideas are generated from students, the librarian provides feedback on how ideas may be further developed, or what else could be added to the concept map to make it most useful.

4. At the end of the session, the librarian provides the concept map assignment to the students and instructions to email the URL to the Prezi to the librarian. If there is enough time in class to work on the projects, students are encouraged to do so before leaving.

5. Upon receipt of the assignments, the librarian reviews the concept maps for content, and provides feedback to the students regarding library resources or research keywords they may want to consider in the future.

ALLERGY WARNINGS

Studio art students may become so wrapped up in the aesthetics of their concept map that they forget to focus on the concept mapping objectives. Offer encouragement to generate as many ideas as possible before focusing on making it look pretty.

CHEF'S NOTE

Students who had this session reacted very positively to both the tool and the feedback given on their assignments. Those who had never used Prezi before were very excited about it, and those who had used it before commented that this was a great new way to think about it. The opportunity to have individual contact with students on their projects is a critical step in ensuring they feel comfortable with the librarian and the library, and will then come to those resources in the future. In addition, such tailored feedback for each student allows for the recommendation of previously undiscovered resources or ideas.

This instructional session may stand on its own, or may be paired with other sessions that further develop the research process. I typically have a session on conceptual research and then one demonstrating library resources for students to use once they have developed research strategies.

ADDITIONAL RESOURCES

- Sample Prezi: http://prezi.com/0fswsuccxdeh/motherhood-a-concept-map/

Building and Tactile Learning in the Literature Classroom

Alison Valk, Multimedia Instructional Librarian, Georgia Institute of Technology, alison.valk@library.gatech.edu; Robin Wharton, Co-Founder and Director, The Calliope Initiative, Inc., Partner and Production Editor, Hybrid Pedagogy, robin.s.wharton@gmail.com

NUTRITION INFORMATION

Understanding and appreciating the affordances of digital media involves understanding and appreciating the affordances of analog media, like the book. In this project for an upper-division seminar on the life and work of Geoffrey Chaucer, rather than asking students to write individual essays on the history of the book, manuscript production, handwriting, and the creation and dissemination of different editions, they were asked to apply their knowledge about all these things to create and digitize their own edition of some of Chaucer's shorter poems. Through a series of workshops facilitated by the embedded librarian, the students synthesized their learning about medieval and contemporary book and manuscript culture to produce handmade and digital artifacts reflecting their insights into Chaucer's work.

The specific approach—working with students to design, fabricate, and digitize a book—would work well in any medieval studies class focused on literature. The general approach—involving students in tactile learning or "building"—would work well for a variety of subject areas that emphasize or focus upon physical processes or artifacts.

We designed this project for an upper-division major authors seminar in a large metropolitan campus. The first stage of the project involved these students in fabricating a manuscript codex of Middle English poetry with critical commentary. The second stage required them to digitize the manuscript and create a website to display the digital version alongside a variety of scholarly resources. One project goal was to link the classroom to other physical and virtual learning spaces on campus and within the community. We completed project work in the library's multimedia instruction lab, the Walter C. Williams Paper Museum, the Artists' Library at the Atlanta campus of the Savannah College of Art and Design, the Georgia Tech craft studio, and a local woodworking shop, among other locations. Students also drew upon a variety of digital resources about manuscript studies, bookbinding, web design, and critical bibliography.

Goal/Purpose

In addition to furthering students' understanding of literature, history, media and communication, this project was also designed to investigate how the study of literature and history can serve as a springboard for creativity. By presenting students with a "problem" for which they had to design a "solution," the project provided an opportunity to consider how the study of alternative methods, processes, and ways of knowing from history might help us in our efforts to "think outside the box" when confronted with contemporary problems. As a byproduct of this process, the students were encouraged to think about non-traditional physical spaces as viable resources for achieving their learning objectives. The students were also interactively engaged in designing their assignment. For instance, students were responsible for the design, content, and materials used in the codex, and the choice of platforms used in creating their website. The project was designed to encourage a sense of ownership over both the end product and process used to reach that end point. Finally, students' collaborative work throughout helped them to develop and hone strategies for communication, cooperation, and evaluation; skills that will be of value beyond the non-academic workplace.

SERVES

15–24 students if you are making one book/one digital edition, 25–40 if you are making two. Beyond 40 students the process might become unmanageable for one librarian and one instructor working together, though it could work for a large-enrollment, lecture + break-out session class as a collaboration among the main instructor of record, the embedded librarian, and the graduate students leading the breakout sessions.

COOKING TIME

Total duration: Roughly 10 weeks out of a 15-week semester
Bookmaking workshop: 3 hours
Papermaking workshop: 50 minutes
Digitization workshop: 2 sessions–50 minutes each
In-class work sessions: 5 sessions–50 minutes each

FIGURE 1. Bookmaking workshop

INGREDIENTS AND EQUIPMENT

- Bookmaking workshop
- Available studio space
- Basic bookmaking supplies (thread, awls, glue, paper, fabric, board)
- Subject specialist—fine arts
- Handouts—tips on the process.
- Camera equipment—optional, to film session.

- Papermaking workshop
- Available studio space
- Basic paper-making supplies (deckle, screens, pulp, sponges)
- Subject specialist—fine arts
- Handouts providing tips on the process

Manuscript Digitization Workshops
- Computer lab with work stations for all students
- Available server space for software setup
- Instances of Omeka and Mediawiki set up for demonstration purposes
- Class slides providing comparison of features
- Multimedia instruction librarian
- Instructor station with projector
- Preparation

Bookmaking Workshop
You will need to locate and reserve appropriate studio space as well as coordinate with any workshop collaborators or assistants. You will need to determine local supply sources or online resources for workshop supplies. Once an approximate supply cost is determined, the instructor should obtain lab fees from the students. The lead instructor for the workshop will want to collect appropriate book binding supplies for each of the students participating. The supplies you purchase will depend on the type of book structure you are creating. Prep your paper and book board by having it pre-cut—it saves time. Create handouts for the students; handouts can be useful in helping students retain key aspects of the process.

Papermaking Workshop
You will need to locate and reserve appropriate studio space as well as coordinate with any workshop collaborators or assistants. Again, you will want to assist in gathering basic supplies for the students. Basic papermaking techniques and supplies would suffice for a project such as this. Workshop collaborators can be of assistance in locating necessary supplies. Create handouts for the students; handouts can be useful in helping students retain key aspects of the process. In our case, the Williams Paper Museum had supplies (wood and screen for constructing frames and deckles, and cotton fiber, water, and sizing for making paper), but one student actually volunteered her time and the shop to which she had access to construct the frames and deckles for this project. The students then made the paper at the museum.

Manuscript Digitization Workshops
You will need to evaluate e-publishing tools and platforms appropriate to class objective/ goals. Narrow your list down to the software options that best fit the class. Prepare a presentation and slides presenting the pros and cons of available platforms. It is always helpful for the students to be able to try out the software, therefore set up test instances of the platform options (in this case Omeka, MediaWiki). Research any supplemental materials such as handbooks or any additional resources you can bring to the workshop. Reserve your classroom space and make sure there is room for small groups to work together. Finally, if you run a

follow up workshop, collect feedback from the students ahead of time regarding specific technical issues so you can tackle them in your second session.

COOKING METHOD
Bookmaking/Binding

1. The bookmaking workshop works out best when you are collaborating with art instructors who specialize in book binding. Not only can these collaborators advise you on supply lists, they can bring their expertise to the classroom.

FIGURE 2. Bound book

2. Determine which of the students have had experience in this area before. This can help the students determine project roles, as well as to let you know which students may need extra assistance in the workshop.
3. Begin the workshop by showing the students examples of various completed book structures.
4. Take the students through the step by step process of creating their own handmade book. This varies greatly depending on the book structure; however there are many resources online which provide thorough instructions on the creation of simple book structures that even a novice can handle! For our workshop, the students created 2 books each; they learned both case binding and the long stitch technique.
5. The students love taking their own handmade books home with them!

FIGURE 3. Chaucer book

Manuscript Digitization

1. The digitization workshop begins with an overview and slide presentation of available platforms in line with project goals. We discuss the pros and cons of each platform. In our case we discussed Omeka and MediaWiki.
2. The instructor will introduce the test instances of the software and provide a demo for the students. Students are given permissions to login and try the software out for themselves.
3. The instructor will demo basic functionality and show the students examples they would likely encounter in their class project. Examples might include how to format text or how to work with images in Media Wiki.
4. It is helpful to have a follow up workshop scheduled. During the second workshop students can receive tailored assistance once the project is underway. This gives the students an opportunity to present the librarian with specific technical problems they may be encountering.

ALLERGY WARNINGS

- Plan activities in advance: Project can be time intensive given the necessary coordination with other facilities and resources on campus.
- Use collaborative virtual workspaces: (a Google Doc, a class wiki) to facilitate brainstorming and coordination. Include librarian, guest subject-matter experts, and instructor in all of these student conversations.
- Be clear on expectations: Need to ensure students are willing to invest necessary time outside of class.
- Provide adequate opportunities for collaboration during class time.
- Supplies for bookmaking are specialized: If students are unfamiliar with the bookmaking process, it's best to provide the students with the supplies and have them pay a class fee, rather than having them collect supplies on their own.
- Bookmaking workshops work better in smaller groups.
- Make sure you have available resources to work with open source software: Necessary server access or colleagues who can assist you with access.

CHEFS' NOTE

This project might work best as a cohesive semester long project, rather than segmented into separate projects, one focused on fabricating the manuscript and one focused on creating a digital edition. Rolling the project of creating a digital edition into the process of creating the physical book would help students understand more about the internal layout and construction of the physical book as well as the advantages and affordances of digital publishing media. When we run the project again, we will experiment with asking students to create a digital version of the book first, before turning to creating the physical artifact, to see if it results in a more polished work product as well as a more effective collaborative process. This project created a valuable opportunity for students and instructors to build connections by collaborating and working creatively with departments all over campus as well as neighboring schools. It also gave students an opportunity to observe how academic communities collaborate in the production of knowledge. Finally, one unanticipated benefit of the process was the ongoing conversation over the course of the project about the fate of both the physical and digital editions after the class was over. The students were genuinely interested in creating artifacts that would be of use to future students and scholars, something that we do not always see with more traditional assignments.

ADDITIONAL RESOURCES

- http://omeka.org/
- http://www.mediawiki.org/wiki/MediaWiki
- http://www.philobiblon.com/tutorials.shtml
- http://www.getty.edu/art/exhibitions/making/
- http://www.thedigitalwalters.org/
- http://auchinleck.nls.uk/
- http://www.digitalbookindex.org/search001a.htm
- http://machias.edu/faculty/necastro/chaucer/
- http://www.dancingpencalligraphy.com/howto/Exercises.html

Primary Source Stew:
Helping Students Create a Historical Narrative Using Primary Sources in the University Archives

Erin Lawrimore, University Archivist, The University of North Carolina at Greensboro, erlawrim@uncg.edu

NUTRITION INFORMATION
We worked with four English 101 instructors to provide primary-source instruction and facilitate use of university archives by first-year students. The first-year students conducted research using primary sources in the university archives to create a short (3–5 page) narrative of a person, event, or other topic in university history. The narrative could take the form of a traditional historical essay or may take a more creative route, such as a graphic novel representation or a fictional speech to be given by a key figure at an historical event.

While this project was incorporated into English 101, it would be easily transferred to an introductory history course or any other class where students can gain value from analyzing multiple primary sources to create a single narrative.

SERVES
Individual class sizes are 26, but could be extended or limited based on number of classes being taught and researcher capacity in the university archives.

LENGTH OF PROJECT
4–6 weeks

INGREDIENTS AND EQUIPMENT
- Archival collections with a basic level of intellectual control, documenting the history of the university.

PREPARATION
- Students completed a general library instructional session.
- Archivist prepared a general list of possible topics (not exhaustive), and created a resource (such as a LibGuide) consolidating links to the various sites for gathering information about archival collections. This should include links to finding aids and digitized university history collections.

COOKING METHOD
We worked with four graduate English 101 instructors (all under the supervision of a tenured faculty member) to use university archives as a ground for first-year students to learn how to critically examine and interpret primary sources, how to conduct archival research, and how to create a single narrative from multiple types of archival records (correspondence, student publications, annual reports, photographs, etc.).

Instructors conducted sessions focused on primary vs. secondary sources. Students were asked to perform a basic primary source document analysis, in which they examined a document's format, creator, audience, function, and message. The archivist provided a presentation on the history of the university, covering a number of major individuals and events from the institution's founding through today. The session was deliberately broad, as it was intended to serve as a launching point for students' individual research projects.

The archivist introduced the class to online resources available for planning your research trip to the university archives. This included instructing the students on how to use archival finding aids to identify the portion of collections that might be useful in research.

The archivist instructed the classes on the best methods for searching and using digitized archival collections, while also stressing that the digitized collections represented only a very small portion of the total holdings of the university archives.

Students selected a topic for their research, working with their instructor and the archivist to select a topic narrow enough to provide a clear route for research while also broad enough to have sufficient representation in the university archives collections.

Students were given one or two class sessions (it varied by instructor) to conduct hands-on research in the university archives. They were also encouraged to return to the university archives independently as needed for further research time.

In their research, students were asked to find records of various formats or records intended for different audiences to provide them with a broader perspective on their chosen topic. For instance, a student working on a biography of the first African-American student on campus might use articles from the student newspaper and the local newspapers, memos from the university chancellor, photographs, and oral history interview to build their narrative. This necessitated using archival finding aids, digitized collections, and the library's general catalog to identify possible sources.

Students wrote a 3–5 page narrative, based on university archives resources, on their chosen topic. They also wrote a brief (1–2 page) follow-up essay, reflecting on their experience in the university archives and the choices that they made in selecting and interpreting archival records.

SUBJECT/DISCIPLINE ADDRESSED
English 101, covering information literacy with a focus on rhetorical analysis

ALLERGY WARNING
The mediated nature of access to the archives could prove problematic, both in terms of logistics (where to put all the students while they conduct research?) and student schedules (with limited hours of operations, how does the university archives accommodate a student who works full-time?). To alleviate the logistical issue, students are referred to digitized resources whenever possible. To accommodate student schedules, the instructor allotted a full class period for archival research.

Communication with the instructor (in this case, graduate students teaching English 101) is key in the planning phase. He or she must understand the nature of archives (mediated research, breadth of the collection, available tools for searching for information about university archives collections, and a realistic view of the time required for the actual archival research). As many instructors themselves have not conducted archival research, it is critical to instruct **them** at the earliest phases of planning the course. The semester before the courses began, instructors were giving an extensive introduction to university archives, finding aids, digitized collections, and other methods and issues related to archival research.

When working with multiple classes on a similar project in the university archives, it may be important to stagger assignment deadlines so that the archivist isn't overwhelmed and unable to properly facilitate the consultations and research times needed.

CHEF'S NOTE
While many students expressed fear or frustration at the nature of archival research, most found the class and this assignment in particular to be a fun opportunity to be creative while also learning more about the university they now attend. So, in addition to encouraging information literacy, this assignment helps first-year students feel more of a sense of ownership in their university and its history. The hope is that this ownership will help enhance student retention by providing them with a sense of community through engagement with the past.

Having "subject files" on popular topics (folders containing newspaper clippings, photocopies of frequently used documents, and other ready reference information) can help students gain a broader understanding of their topic needed to conduct targeted archival research.

Ideally, you will have some of the major campus publications, like the yearbooks or student newspapers, in multiple copies or available online or on microfilm. These resources will be used by most, if not all, of the students, so availability is important. Accessibility of additional copies outside of university archives (either online or as part of the general library or general reference collections) will allow students to continue research beyond the university archives' more limited hours of operation. The reflective essays from the students can prove valuable in planning for this project in future semester. Issues encountered by the students in one semester might be avoided in following semesters with an adjustment by the instructors or the archivist.

This is an on-going project, with a number of new English 101 classes returning to the university archives each semester. The tenured faculty member who supervised the multi-class project plans to gather the best essays produced each semester, and compile them into an e-book publication that can be used as a way for other new students to learn about important people or events in university history.

INSTRUCTIONAL RESOURCES
- LibGuide created for this project: http://uncg.libguides.com/eng101archives

Cookin' Up State and Local Government Research

Connie James-Jenkin, Elgin Community College, cjames- jenkin@elgin.edu; Stacey Shah, Elgin Community College, sshah@elgin.edu

NUTRITION INFORMATION

The setting for this recipe was a community college 100-level political science online course, State and Local Government. Students select a topic of state/local importance and research and write a semester-long paper. They must use a variety of sources, including scholarly journals. Integrate information literacy instruction throughout the research paper process.

SERVES

Up to 30

COOKING TIME

8–10 weeks

INGREDIENTS AND EQUIPMENT

- Access to Learning Management System
- Tutorial software (we used Captivate/YouTube)
- LibGuides, Google Drive
- An instructor who values information literacy and is eager to collaborate with librarians

PREPARATION

Concocted tutorials, LibGuide links to sources, Google Drive Librarian Consultation Form

Tutorials

Created using Captivate and then uploaded to YouTube

1. "Researching State and Local Topics" teaches how to look at the big picture of a topic, then search for it on a local level. Discusses appropriate databases to search.
2. "Simple Search Strategies" teaches how to effectively search library databases by selecting keywords, Boolean searching, refining searches.
3. "Why and When to Cite Your Sources" discusses the importance and reasons to cite sources. Also discusses using Chicago Manual of Style for this class.
4. "Cost/Benefit Analysis" Created in collaboration with the instructor

LibGuide

5. Created a general library/research LibGuide for Distance Learning students for completion in the first 2 weeks of class.
6. Created a customized class research guide linking to tutorials, appropriate databases, websites

Google Doc Form

Students must complete a librarian consultation form. We created the form using a Google Doc form, and embedded it into the LibGuide

METHOD

Add different ingredients on a weekly basis. Start by adding librarian introductions to the class. When the paper is assigned in week two, begin adding tutorials, and links to appropriate sources. Toss in a librarian consultation mid-project. Allow ingredients to simmer with the students as they write their paper. Top off with tutorial on citing.

ALLERGY WARNING

All the librarian consultations tend to come in at the same time. Be prepared to enlist sous-chefs if needed!

CHEFS' NOTE

This class really integrates information literacy and library instruction throughout the semester. With different assignments and expectations throughout the semester, the librarians have lots of interactions with the students. The librarians are able to work with and guide students through the entire research process from topic selection to finalizing citations.

5. Al Fresco Dining: Embedding in Online Courses

One of the biggest areas of growth for embedded librarians is the world of online coursework. The Learning Management System (LMS) provides a fertile location for a librarian to take up residence over time and to embed scalable services and learning objects. By joining the LMS discussion, you can become a true member of the classroom community and share library content over time. A little advance planning will allow you to provide research support online in a scalable fashion. Many librarians have developed strategies to embed in the LMS, and they share their best practices in this section. Whatever your LMS, and whether your classes are 100% online or a hybrid of face-to-face and online learning, these recipes provide excellent tips and ideas for embedding in online environments.

Feed Them When They're Hungry:
Embedding in an Online Asynchronous Graduate Level Research and Writing Course

Qiana Johnson, Schaffner and Distance Learning, Northwestern University, q-johnson@northwestern.edu

NUTRITION INFORMATION

This is a hearty dish that comes from embedding in this particular type of class to provide research assistance at the point of need. The librarian can answer student research questions even when they don't realize they are asking "library" questions.

SERVES

15 students online

COOKING TIME

2 to 3 weeks or the entire quarter. The librarian and faculty member can work together to determine if there is a core time where students may particularly need assistance or if it would be best to have the librarian engaged for the entire quarter.

INGREDIENTS AND EQUIPMENT

A dedicated discussion board within a course's Learning Management System (LMS) site, as well as a sprinkling of librarian-supplied information in other discussion boards for flavor.

PREPARATION

This recipe requires establishing a close working relationship with the teaching faculty member. The faculty member (or the LMS administrator) adds you as a teaching assistant. This allows you to see and post to discussion boards and post links to the site, but it doesn't give you full access to the site. You or the faculty member can set up a dedicated "library discussion board." This board allows students to post their questions and get feedback from a librarian. The discussion board is also the place where students can highlight research successes or difficulties that they run into. This provides the opportunity for individual students to get assistance, but also allows other students in the class to see the answer and apply it to their own research. The librarian should also monitor other discussion boards within the course site.

While having one dedicated board for library questions can be helpful, questions that could benefit from a librarian perspective may come up on other boards. If the librarian is a fully integrated member of the class, the librarian provides feedback in these other forums. This again will provide answers to a single student, and also provide the information to a larger audience.

The librarian should provide a collection of suggested accompaniments in the form of course links. These links can be to appropriate research guides, online tutorials and videos, information about how to get reference help, etc. As questions come up through the discussion boards, other relevant links can be added.

COOKING METHOD

The librarian checks the discussion boards at least once a day. If it is possible, checking the boards once in the morning and once in the afternoon is preferred. The librarian answers library/research specific questions as they come up. He or she also provides feedback in other areas as appropriate. For example, if on a discussion forum about conducting literature reviews, a student mentions that they have difficulty determining if a journal is peer-reviewed or not, the librarian can share resources students can use to locate information about a journal.

Some students are uncomfortable asking questions in such a public forum and may choose to email or call the librarian directly. This isn't a problem with the recipe—merely a different way tasters experience it. Direct contact can allow the librarian to see some commonly occurring questions and create a post about them without the question being linked to any one student.

Strong communication with the faculty member is important during the quarter, especially if absences are anticipated due to vacations or conference attendance. Known absences can be entered on a calendar or made as an announcement to allow students to plan their research.

ALLERGY WARNINGS

This can be a very rewarding project, but it can also be very time-consuming. In some cases, different students will ask similar questions because they are not reading the responses to questions of other students. Often when that happens, the faculty member encourages the students, through a message to all the students, to read previous responses to other questions. A single librarian could handle two, possibly three classes. However, more than that becomes unmanageable. Because of that, this recipe is not as scalable as others and is more suited to intimate groups. If requests increase beyond what library staff can appropriately manage, guidelines may need to be developed addressing what types of classes lend themselves best to this type of embedded librarian experience.

CHEF'S NOTE

While being embedded in a class this way is helpful to the students, it is equally helpful to the librarian. This project allows the librarian to see common areas that students struggle with, where they start their research, why they are starting there, and where they feel library resources are fail-

ing them. This project provides an excellent bird's eye view of how students conduct their research. This project also encourages librarians to develop and use new tools to answer questions. While embedded in a course, there are times when the librarian is not there. Tools such as videos, handouts, or web site guides can provide assistance when library staff is not there. Regular interactions on the discussion boards also allow students (and faculty) to become more familiar with you. This familiarity can lead to future interactions outside of the class you embed with.

Pathways Potluck:
They Bring the Questions, We Bring the Research!

Beth Filar Williams, University of North Carolina at Greensboro, efwilli3@uncg.edu; Jenny Dale, University of North Carolina at Greensboro, jedale2@uncg.edu

NUTRITION INFORMATION

Our goal is to assist students in finding appropriate scholarly sources for their final research papers in an entry level (Pathways) course for the BA in Liberal Studies. We have been invited to work with this class to help students in the online Humanities program develop and hone their information literacy skills and become more familiar with library services and resources for distance students.

SERVES

20–25 students in an online course.

COOKING TIME

Prep time: At start of each semester update the LibGuide and touching base with the professor.

Cooking time: The bulk of the work is concentrated at key times during mid-semester when research paper assignment is due.

INGREDIENTS AND EQUIPMENT

Your brain and a computer with an Internet connection!

PREPARATION

- Identify the entry level course for an online program with a research need.

- Meet with the professor to discuss the syllabus, goals, assignments, etc.
- Explain how librarians can help with research assignments.
- Get the professor to add the librarian(s) as course builders or TAs in the course

shell in the learning management system and have professor encourage students to consult with librarians at the time of research paper assignment.
- Set up a LibGuide for the class to use that includes relevant library resources

FIGURE 1. Embedded librarian email to student

Jenny Dale <jedale2@uncg.edu>   10/23/11
to Alyson, Beth

Hi Alyson,

Thank you for getting in touch with us! It sounds like you've chosen a really interesting research topic.

I've done a bit of searching and here are a few tips I have for getting started:

1. Use the MLA International Bibliography. If you visit the BLS 301 Course Guide (library homepage - research guides by subject - Liberal Studies - BLS 301), there's a link to this database on the Research Paper tab. This is one of our main sources for literary research. I'd recommend pulling out the most important concepts in your search - probably Hard Times, structure, and biblical connection. I tried a search with Hard Times in the top search box and bibl* in the one below it. The little * serves as a truncation symbol. By doing bibl* instead of biblical, the database knows to search bible, biblical, and anything else that starts with that root.

2. One of the challenges of literature research is that there's often not an article or book out there that says exactly what you want it to say. You usually have to be creative and pull together sources that support your argument. In your case, for instance, you might find articles that deal with religious overtones in Hard Times rather than specific biblical connections. You can still build your argument by using those. You may also find works that deal with Dickens more broadly as a writer, and maybe don't focus strictly on Hard Times. Those could have good support for you, too.

3. The library catalog is another good place to check - you can do keyword searches there to find books or chapters in books. We have a good collection of literary criticism on 19th Century British Literature, and plenty of criticism and interpretation of Dickens' works.

I hope this helps you get started. Please let me know if you need me to clarify anything, and keep me posted about how I can help as you're working through your research. I'm always happy to help by email, phone, chat, or in person. Just let me know!

Thanks and best,
Jenny

and databases as well as information about services for distance learners.

- Record a video greeting to students to help them personally connect with the librarian ("we are real people!"). Embed video in LibGuide and in Blackboard course.

COOKING METHOD

During course, push announcements to students at key times when assignments are due and periodically check on discussion boards or set up notifications. During research paper assignment, students will email librarian(s) once their professor has approved their research topic.

Create a template email response that can be tweaked for each student since most will start with the same handful of databases and copy each other on the email if more than one librarian is embedded. (See Figure 1.) Let the professor know which students have consulted with the librarians. At end of semester, reflect with professor and possibly review papers for assessment.

ALLERGY WARNINGS

It is critical to collaborate with faculty to ensure that there is a relevant and appropriate research project. This idea is best for the entry class for an online only degree program, otherwise it is not scalable to all courses due to the time involved. Consultations can take 15–30 minutes for each student, and sometimes more if they come back with more questions.

CHEFS' NOTE

At the end of each semester, it is important to reflect on how the embedded project worked. Each class is different, and some semesters are more successful than others. Active reflection and periodic check-ins with the course instructor help ensure a successful embedded relationship between the librarian and the students in the course.

ADDITIONAL RESOURCES

- Course LibGuide available at http://uncg.libguides.com/bls301

FIGURE 2. Embedded Librarians Guide

The Slow-Baked Ham of Integrated Librarianship:
Getting into Online Learning Spaces with Limited Resources

Heather Lamond, Head of Distance Library Service, Massey University Library, h.m.lamond@massey.ac.nz; Elizabeth Chisholm, Planning and Quality Librarian, Massey University Library, e.chisholm@massey.ac.nz

NUTRITION INFORMATION

Developed for distance students whose only on-campus experience was a 1–2 day residential course early in their study. The residential courses are packed with curriculum content and very intensive.

Our goal was to design a model which was going to allow a small library team to enable learners to develop information literacy skills where and when they need them in an online environment. It was important that the learning was authentic, and gave the learner choice to construct their own knowledge from their current level of understanding. It needed to deliver a learning experience that was equivalent to, if not better than, the learning in a face-to-face class.

SERVES

Groups of 10–120 students in online classes, including distance and adult learners.

COOKING TIME

This recipe takes a little bit of preparation and the cooking needs to be well thought out (so it is not a quick stirfry!), but once you've done the preparation and cooking, it works well for a long time.

The module is placed at the point in the paper where most students will start the information-finding process, but it can be completed or referred back to at any time during their course. The student spends the amount of time required to gain the skills (estimate 45 minutes–one hour, and at the completion of tasks students should have found information for their current assignment).

INGREDIENTS AND EQUIPMENT
- Editing access to the Learning Management System (LMS)
- A suite of reusable learning objects
- 1.5 FTE professional librarians

PREPARATION

Strong marketing and promotion of the model to faculty with the key message is that this is a better way of doing things for the learner (at point of need and a good use of the learner's time).

Work with the faculty member to understand the assignments to enable targeting the point of need for developing IL skills. Library content is integrated into the curriculum material and teaching faculty highlight it at the point where it is of most use.

Faculty also need to provide a citation or a relevant journal article for learners to find that will be useful in their learning. This is the basis for one of the authentic tasks.

The model can be easily adapted for use in many courses without significant tailoring and this should be kept in mind when working with faculty and preparing for each course. Plan to use material already available (e.g. learning objects) and use a template for the library module which highlights the few course specific segments (e.g. assignment topic, journal article citation or database choice). For future courses it is only these segments that need adapting.

TECHNIQUE/ COOKING METHOD
1. List learning outcomes/objectives and how these would be measured.
2. Create a "teaching plan" for the online module—this creates the basic template for the module.
3. Use the LMS to create containers for the information literacy module at the most effective point in their course. (We used a Moodle book but this is easily substituted with an alternative ingredient).
4. Provide an opportunity for the learner to ascertain their current understand-

ing and then provide a choice to either refresh their understanding or move on.

5. Determine the "pain points" in assignment preparation or research, and concentrate the learning at that stage and on that subject (e.g. choosing a search tool and developing search terms).

6. Within the course material embed the library module (including online learning objects) that demonstrates the skills students need to get past that "pain point." After viewing the demonstration, learners are asked to apply the skills to find useful information for their assignments through authentic learning tasks.

7. Set up discussion forums for students to respond to learning tasks—answers or comments. Librarians post responses as needed to give guidance and encouragement. Note: while librarians respond to the first post in a forum, not all posts require a response. Only respond where necessary to guide and remember that one response will reach all students in the course, thereby saving time.

8. Measure student engagement with the library content through participation reports within the LMS. These provide us with statistics of views of the Moodle book and forum and the number of posts in forums. We record a student's viewing of the book and the forum (whether they've viewed them once or numerous times) and we record if they have posted. Gather qualitative feedback from the discussion forums for evidence-based development of further modules.

FIGURE 1: An example of the template for the LMS—highlights on the right indicate the parts that need tailoring for specific courses. Navigation on the left shows the extent of the content.

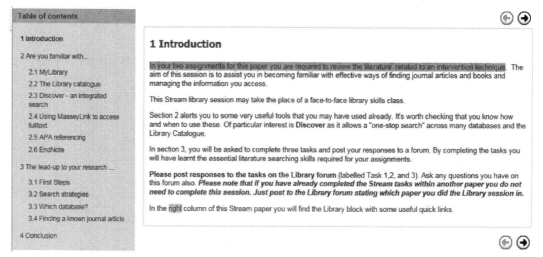

ALLERGY WARNINGS

Don't be concerned about not being able to keep up with discussion forum postings. If you take the time to word the task so that there is no right or wrong answer, but rather so that you can get an idea if the learner is on the right track then you are not tied up with marking responses. Therefore, you don't need to respond to every posting. Remember that one response will reach all participants and as they often struggle at the same pain points, this is effective communication.

Placement of the module and faculty encouragement of the learners is critical to getting engagement with the module.

A lack of forum postings doesn't necessarily mean low engagement, remember to measure viewing of the material as well.

Spend time and energy working on the courses where you are needed—not every course requires the learners to develop or use IL skills and the relevance of the module is again critical to engagement.

CHEFS' NOTE

Faculty in the Institute of Education appreciated the freeing up of time in their busy residential courses. We received faculty endorsement on the pedagogy and on the model used from faculty who are experts in education.

Learner endorsement included statements like "wish I'd had this earlier in my study," and other responses in forums show that the learning objectives were achieved.

Librarians' point of view: it is heartening to feel that students put in the amount of time

FIGURE 2. Example of a reusable online learning objects used in the module

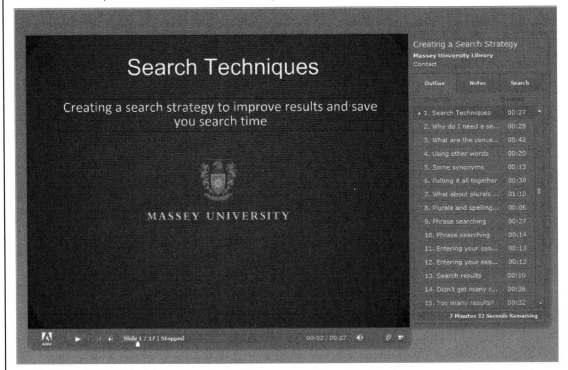

used in 40 Education courses. For 2013 the model is business as usual for the Institute of Education.

ADDITIONAL RESOURCES

- Massey University Library Online Learning Objects http://www.massey.ac.nz/massey/research/library/help-and-instruction/how-to-find/show-me-how-masterlist/show-me-how-masterlist_home.cfm

- Chisholm, E. M. & Lamond, H. M.. (2012). Information Literacy Development at a Distance: Embedded or Reality? *Journal Of Library & Information Services In Distance Learning*, 6 (3/4), 224. doi:10.1080/153329 0X.2012.705170

they needed or wanted to develop these skills, and not what was blocked out in a timetable by faculty or librarians with no knowledge of their current skills and abilities.

Students appreciate that this module allows them to work at their own pace and to spend as much or as little time as they need to gain the needed information skills and that we are acknowledging their previous experience and skills—making for a constructivist learning experience.

Forum postings were not onerous and allowed relationships to be built online that wouldn't be otherwise. Learners engaged because they were in control and not stuck in a class at the end of a long day.

Tasks are an absolutely essential ingredient of the recipe and must be included to ensure learning is achieved. Learners have a tendency to gloss over information literacy material and assume they have the knowledge already, but only by doing the authentic tasks is true understanding achieved.

We taste tested the recipe in 2010 in five courses. Then added to the menu and marketed widely in 2011 and by 2012 was

Brunch with a Side of Hashtags

Melissa Mallon, Coordinator of Library Instruction, Wichita State University, melissa.mallon@wichita.edu,
twitter: @librarianliss

NUTRITION INFORMATION
The setting for this embedded strategy is entirely online served over a bed of social networking.

FIGURE 1: Embedded Librarian Hashtags

The method of embedding discussed in this recipe has a librarian follow and engage with a specific course via a Twitter hashtag. Face-to-face library instruction sessions are not possible for many classes for a variety of reasons. For example, a class might meet online, or the course schedule might not allow for a librarian to attend. However, the librarian likely has valuable information to teach the students. Thus enters the hashtag (words tagged with a # sign at the end of tweets). Like the essential brunch food hashbrowns, hashtags are a very important part of Twitter.

Librarians can use a course hashtag to send students articles, research tips, and more throughout the semester or during a specific research project. Instructors and students can also post tweets tagged with the course hashtag, using this method as a way to engage with one another and the librarian. Since all interaction is done online, via Twitter, instructors will not have to give up valuable class time for research instruction.

SERVES
This recipe feeds a crowd. The use of hashtags allows the librarian to interact with a large number of students in a virtual environment. See additional information regarding following students on Twitter under "Allergy Warning" below.

COOKING TIME
Cooking time can vary. For the librarian cooking a large brunch, following a hashtag may last an entire semester. For librarians and instructors wishing to offer students a more low-key, cereal type experience, the interaction may only span as little as a week or two, or the time it takes for students to complete a research assignment.

INGREDIENTS AND EQUIPMENT
- Twitter account

- Social media account manager, such as Hootsuite or Tweetdeck (optional)

PREPARATION
Prior to the start of the embedded project, the librarian will need to work with the course instructor to design a hashtag. The hashtag should incorporate the course theme or number, and possibly something university-related, to set it apart from other hashtags. The librarian should search Twitter for the hashtag to make sure it is not already taken. Examples of hashtags for classes I've been embedded in include #wsusm (Wichita State University Social Media, for a communication class) and #wsusales (Wichita State University Sales, for a marketing class). Another example comes from a human resources class and uses the course number: #hrm666.

COOKING METHOD
This recipe is suitable for librarians of all types, including those who are hesitant about using social media. Embedded librarians need not be Twitter experts, but some familiarity with the tool does help.

FIGURE 2: Tweet by @librarianliss

Melissa Mallon @librarianliss   29 Oct
Twitter-Journalism (Twittalism): What Are the Responsibilities of the Academic Live-Tweeter? | HASTAC hastac.org/blogs/amanda-s...
#wsusm
Expand

Once the librarian determines the hashtag and the timeline for embedding with the instructor, they are ready to start tweeting. It may be helpful to whisk up a bowl of tips and relevant resources at the beginning of the semester and spread them out over the course of the embedded project. This technique will keep the librarian from feeling overwhelmed, and will help confirm they have found an adequate amount of content to share. The librarian should also watch the hashtag regularly to make sure student questions are being answered or addressed.

This activity works best with classes that have been introduced to, and even required to use social networks, such as a communication or marketing course. Other course instructors can easily be encouraged to add Twitter to their cuisine with a short recipe book or instructional tutorial on setting up a Twitter account and using hash tags.

ALLERGY WARNINGS
Depending on the number of students in the course, this method could be akin to eating too many pancakes: overload and the desire to go back to bed. If the embedded librarian follows all of the students, the volume of tweets can be overwhelming, especially if the instructor has required students to tweet. The librarian can avoid this by following the hashtag, rather than the students' accounts. However, a word of warning: if a student follows you, they can be hurt or disappointed if you do not follow them back.

A secondary caution depends on how the librarian uses his or her Twitter account. If it is for personal use only, a secondary "embedded librarian" account is a good idea. This separate account could be used only for the purpose of course-related tweets.

CHEF'S NOTE
Overall, this is an effective and quick way to connect with students and share up-to-date resources and research tips with students in a course. I had assumed I would also answer reference questions via the course hashtag, and while I could provide some information, I often found myself needing to email students with a complete answer due to Twitter's 140 character limit.

I found that my Twitter interactions with students created much more of a bond than one-shot library instruction sessions. You are afforded a glimpse into students' real lives, and vice versa. I have kept in touch with several former students via Twitter, and even answered a reference question for a student working in his first job.

ADDITIONAL RESOURCES
- Twitter: http://twitter.com
- Hootsuite: http://hootsuite.com
- Tweetdeck: http://www.tweetdeck.com

Presentation is Everything:
Creating an Online Personal Profile

Julie Cornett, Instruction Librarian, Cerro Coso Community College, jcornett@cerrocoso.edu

NUTRITION INFORMATION

Requiring new online students to develop their online Learning Management System (LMS)-profile allows for critical thinking and reflection regarding how they present themselves online and leads to discussions about privacy and information ethics as well as authority and credibility.

SERVES

Serves a class of 15–35 undergraduate students who are new to taking online courses.

COOKING TIME

One week

INGREDIENTS AND EQUIPMENT

- Personal profile software (embedded in courseware or web-based)
- Screenshot software (like Jing or Camtasia)
- Time to monitor discussion forum several times throughout week or unit (optional)

PREPARATION

- Obtain permission to collaborate with the course instructor to embed assignment and possible forum into online class.
- Create tutorial/lecture on how to edit profile to embed in class.

- Create librarian personal profile on LMS as an example for students to follow.

COOKING METHOD

1. Librarian is added as a guest instructor with editing privileges to the online class during the week the instructor offers the assignment (first week is best) and is introduced to the class.
2. Librarian adds tutorial/lecture to the weekly content, in collaboration with the instructor, that outlines steps in editing one's personal profile, including (but not limited to): uploading an image (not necessarily a face shot—can be anything the student identifies with) and writing a short bio. Tutorial/lecture includes tips and directions about what type of personal information is appropriate for a college-level personal profile (security and privacy), use of images online (ethics and copyright), and can even include a blurb on "authority" and "credibility" in a world where everyone is an author. Comparisons can be made with social media personal profile creation and maintenance.
3. As an assignment, students edit their personal profiles to include an image and a short biography.

4. The librarian and/or instructor will develop a prompt for an asynchronous discussion forum that asks students to reflect on the process of creating their profiles and comment on others' profiles. To scale topic to social media in general, forum prompt might also ask students about their use of social media—what they post and share, why, what they know about privacy settings on Facebook, etc.
5. Librarian and/or instructor will moderate forum over several days, asking questions such as: Why does online privacy matter? Should students have the same "free speech" protections in college online forums that they do using Facebook?

ALLERGY WARNINGS

Depending on the LMS, profile editing can be advanced. Make sure you are knowledgeable about all the options so you can tailor your instruction and field questions. Also, ensure the support of the LMS specialist on campus to direct students to if they encounter technical glitches.

Because of the reflective nature of the discussion, students can often go "off topic", which is why moderating the discussion board is important.

FIGURE 1. Librarian Personal Profile for the LMS

Julie Cornett

Profile | Edit profile | Forum posts | Blog | Notes | Activity reports

Hi! I'm Julie Cornett, the Librarian at Cerro Coso. I'm looking forward to assisting you with your research assignments.

I work primarily at the IWV campus Library; however, I frequently join online classes to help assist students with course-specific research...so, you'll probably see me again in a future class.

Country: United States
City/town: Ridgecrest
Phone: 760-384-6132
Email address: jcornett@cerrocoso.edu ✉
Web page: http://www.melodicalperiodical.wordpress.com
Skype ID: junocorn
Courses: Pedagogy and Technology Committee, ADMJ-C121-31879-Community Relations, CHDV-C203-31954-Practicum - Field Experience, CHEM-C101-31959-Introduction to Chemistry, CHEM-C113-31960 / CHEM-C113H-31961-General Inorganic Chemistry II, ENGL-C040-32031-Improving Basic Writing Skills, ENGL-C040-32032-Improving Basic Writing Skills, ENGL-C070-32040-Introductory Composition, ENGL-C070-32403-Introductory Composition, ENGL-C101-32046-Freshman Composition, ENGL-C151-32055-Technical Communication, IC-C075-32133-Intro Library Research/Bibliog, Library Instruction Moodle
First access: Tuesday, 25 October 2011, 05:16 PM (1 year 195 days)
Last access: Wednesday, 8 May 2013, 03:13 PM (1 sec)
Roles: Teacher
Interests: mountain biking, singing, gardening, Reading

CHEF'S NOTE

This embedded experience can reveal how well students understand privacy and information ethics and can lead to discussions about the importance of evaluating online information in a world full of social media contributors and online authors. Students also discover that the librarian's knowledge extends beyond simply information access.

Students' online profiles follow them to their other online classes, so creating an effective profile early in their academic career will serve them well in the future.

Tip: Make sure the collaboration with the instructor extends to grading and assessment.

Taste Testing Scholarly and Popular Content to Learn about Authority and Information Context

Elizabeth Leonard, Director, Online Campus Library, Berkeley College, ezl@berkeleycollege.edu

NUTRITION INFORMATION

Undergraduate students will learn to distinguish between the quality of information resources and to place information in proper sociopolitical and historical context.

Serves up to 25 undergraduate students.

COOKING TIME

Recipe designed to braise over five day period; cooking time can be condensed for longer/shorter periods.

INGREDIENTS AND EQUIPMENT

- Access to Learning Management System (LMS)
- Screencast/tutorial software (Adobe Captivate, Camtasia, Articulate Storyline, etc).

PREPARATION

The success of the recipe is dependent on the chemical reaction between the scholarly and popular information, taking into account the chemistry of historical setting, authority, and sociopolitical context.

- Find a peer reviewed article from your digital collection that responds to a research question determined by you and the professor (In our case: "Are women more risk averse than men?")
- Create or re-use a tutorial on "Evaluating Internet Sources." (see "additional resources" below).

COOKING METHOD

What is important in adapting this assignment is to present a research question that both engenders opinions by bloggers and non-scholarly writers and also has published peer reviewed research. Try to avoid "hot button" topics (e.g., abortion, homosexuality), that have belief system based opinions. Students should be engaged, not angry. Try to choose a topic that has multiple opinions and may have even changed over time, due to culture or politics. Other possible topics:

- Are people smarter than they were 100 years ago (lead in to the Flynn Effect)
- Artificial sweeteners—good or bad?
- Is standardized testing in school helpful or deleterious to students?

I have found it best to have this assignment as a Weekly Discussion Topic in the Forum. It will work best if the faculty member (a) makes the assignment mandatory and grades it, (b) participates in the discussion. Otherwise you are seen as a week-long substitute teacher and ignored. While it may be tempting to place the video in the Course Materials section of the Online Course, students are more likely to use it if it is placed in the Discussion Forum, at point of need.

Check the discussion at least once a day, if not more, and expect many last minute posts (if the posts are due on Friday, most will be posted on Friday at 11:30 p.m.). If your institution allows, I suggest posting the first response by Tuesday or Wednesday of the week and the responses to your (or other students') posts by Friday of the week. Despite the asynchronous nature of the course, students still expect quickly answered questions.

I have also found it helpful to keep a copy of the answers you post to students on your computer. Many students ask the same questions but don't generally read each other's posts unless required. Even then, they may not find the Q&A that is relevant to their question, so they just ask it again. If you keep a copy of your answers, you can copy and paste it from your master document rather than retyping.

Be sure to use warm, informal language. Formal writing comes off as impersonal and cold, and intimidates students.

FIGURE 1. Message Board Post Analyzing and Comparing Two Articles

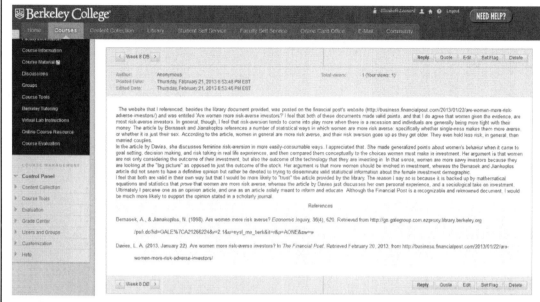

FIGURE 2. Second Example of a Student Message Board Post

ALLERGY WARNINGS

Students may meander off the topic. You will likely need to remind them to stay on topic. Students also struggle to separate their personal opinions from the (possibly) contradictory facts presented by the information sources. You will need to encourage them to post or repost based on the information sources.

CHEF'S NOTE

This was a highly successful and popular assignment. Many students considered the effect of culture, history, and political standing on one's opinions. The students also noted that, while the library article we used was peer reviewed and based on studies, it was also almost 15 years old, and that a similar study taken today might have different outcomes. I was also able to show students that the sources of some articles students provided was NOT the URL of the website (in one example, students found an unpublished working paper stored on the Forbes website and thought it had been published by forbes.com). Additionally, I was able to discuss authority, and point out that some of the authors of Internet material had no background or education in the financial sector, and might not be the most authoritative source to consider.

ADDITIONAL RESOURCES

I branded this Open Source Cooperative Library Instruction Project (CLIP) tutorial: http://www.clip-infolit.org/tutorials/evaluating-internet-resources with my college logo (acceptable under the Creative Commons Copyright). Editing is possible with Abobe Captivate. My version is available at: http://www.screencast.com/t/vc7cTPtm.

Slow-Cooked Embedded Services

Valerie Knight, Reference Librarian, Wayne State College, vaknigh1@wsc.edu; Charissa Loftis, Reference Librarian, Wayne State College, chlofti1@wsc.edu

FIGURE 1. Chef librarians Valerie Knight and Charissa Loftis cook up library instruction.

NUTRITION INFORMATION

Waiting for students to ask questions in the online environment is not ideal and often does not work as well as one might want. Instead, providing tips related to specific assignments as students are working on those assignments will increase student understanding and usage of resources.

COOKING TIME

Slow cooked all semester: sixteen weeks on low for a regular semester or four-eight weeks on high for a summer session.

SERVES

Any size class, 1–50+

INGREDIENTS AND EQUIPMENT

- Learning Management Software (LMS) with forum/bulletin board and email/message system
- Calendar
- Jing or other screen capture software (optional)
- Microphone (optional)
- An online course assigned to you
- Contact information for instructor
- Syllabus and assignments
- Knowledge of available library resources and services
- Knowledge of appropriate resources outside the library

PREPARATION

1. Obtain information about the course(s) assigned to you as an embedded librarian (course number and description; instructor contact information, etc.).
2. Contact the instructor. Ask them about the research needs for the course, assignments, expectations of student work, the desired amount of librarian involvement. Obtain a copy of the syllabus and course assignments.
3. Inform the instructor of your role and limitations in the course (ex. ability to grade library specific assignments, etc.).
4. Review the syllabus and assignments.
   » Match assignments with appropriate virtual and physical information resources.
   » Identify other areas of opportunity to assist beyond the assignments.
   » *Examples: Beowulf* availability as a free e-book; work-arounds for quirks of your LMS
   » Pay attention to assignment due dates. Determine the best time to introduce tips to students.
   » *Examples:* A twenty-page research paper might require steps along the way throughout the semester, whereas a two-page paper might need one or two tips two weeks before it's due.
5. Create a timeline for your own use on your preferred calendar. Note any large gaps in proposed contact times. Plan to touch base with students during the gaps to remind them that you are still available.

COOKING METHOD
Creating Tips

Tips are based on resources and areas of opportunity that you have determined best fit the assignment or course. More than one tip may be needed to explain the research process for a particular assignment. All tips need a brief written introduction.

There are three variations of tips. The type of tip you choose is dependent upon the type of information you need to relay.

1. **Text only**—provides brief content. *Examples:* your personal introduction; direct response to a specific question
2. **Text with links or attachments**—consists of user friendly resources requiring little to no explanation. *Examples*: lists; handouts; links to resources outside the library
3. **Text with video**—a visual walk-through of a more complicated resource (utilize Jing or other screen capture software and microphone if you have one). *Examples*: database and library catalog tips

Posting Tips

Timing is everything! Try to anticipate when the students will be working on the assignment. Post your tip at that time or just before. With lengthy/research intensive projects, you may need to release individual tips that cover different components of research over a longer period of time.

Determining where to post your tips should be given due consideration. Most LMS systems provide a variety of avenues for the delivery of information. If forums or discussion boards are already in use by the instructor, this is an ideal place to post your tips. Ask the instructor to provide you with your own discussion board that is independent from other class discussions. This keeps all library content in one area making it easier to direct students to tips at a later date.

Some LMS systems provide an internal message system that may or may not link to the students' personal email. Using this method allows you to deliver content directly to the student. However, your messages are intermixed with all other messages from course participants making it difficult to relocate tips at a later date.

An effective methodology would be to use both. Post your tips in the forum/discussion board and use the message feature to post reminders.

Interaction with Students

At the beginning of the course you should provide students with multiple avenues to contact you (email, LMS message system, forum, office location, and phone) and your available hours. When a student contacts you there are a variety of ways to respond. If the answer will pertain only to the specific student develop a tip based on one of the three tip variations and send it directly to the student via a message. However, if you feel that more students would benefit from the tip, this is an appropriate time to respond through the forum or a message to the whole group.

ALLERGY WARNINGS

It is important to know your audience. Undergraduate students have different needs than graduate students. Undergraduates need guidance on the basics of research while graduate students frequently want a personal research assistant to guide them through more complex research projects. Librarians should also be aware of age differences and generational gaps that may affect students differently, especially in regards to technology. Location can also impact the type of assistance provided depending on whether students have access to physical resources at the library.

Keep the text of tips short. The resources should be the star! Also, using messages to deliver all tips in short summer courses can be overwhelming and a real irritant to students.

CHEF'S NOTE

One of the best outcomes of the embedded program is that you can walk students through every step of the research process without interrupting instruction time. The program also provides outreach to instructors who in turn can reinforce library resources and services when students don't make good use of the information.

ADDITIONAL RESOURCES

Knight, V. R., & Loftis, C. "Moving from Introverted to Extraverted Embedded Librarian Services: An Example of a Proactive Model." *Journal Of Library & Information Services In Distance Learning*, 6, no. 3/4 (2012): 362–375.

An Annotated Bibliography Medley

Megan McGuire, eLearning Librarian, Mesa Community College, megan.mcguire@mesacc.edu; Serene Rock, Instruction Librarian, Scottsdale Community College, serene.rock@scottsdalecc.edu

NUTRITION INFORMATION

Students will learn to search and find a variety of sources including books, articles, websites, streaming videos, and more. Using the social bookmarking site Diigo, students will select appropriate sources for an annotated bibliography and work collaboratively to evaluate each other's sources for credibility and authority, to summarize each source, and to explain how that source supports their research.

COOKING TIME

A semester long meal, but can be modified into an appetizer or snack.

INGREDIENTS AND EQUIPMENT

- Computer with Internet access
- Diigo account

PREPARATION

Create lessons for each week. Will need to create and/or re-purpose videos and tutorials on some of the topics. Topics include:

- Selecting and refining a topic
- Using Diigo to bookmark sources and collaborate with group members
- Information sources and differentiating between popular and scholarly sources
- Research process

- Evaluating and citing sources
- Search tools and tips such as keywords and Boolean operators
- Searching the catalog, databases, and the Internet for sources
- Creating annotated bibliographies

These lessons can be embedded into a course Learning Management System (LMS) and should include videos, tutorials, instructor notes, etc.

> **FIGURE 1.** Weekly Outline
> Week 1 — Choosing a topic
> Week 2 — Research process and using Diigo
> Week 3 — Information sources & popular versus scholarly sources
> Week 4 — Evaluating & citing sources
> Week 5 — Using search tools
> Week 6 — Using Library Catalog to find books, ebooks, and streaming videos
> Week 7 — Using Library Databases to find articles
> Week 8 — Using the Internet to find web sources
> Week 9 — Choose best sources & edit annotations
> Week 10— Turn in annotated bibliography

COOKING METHOD

Students will access the online materials for each week's lesson and will complete the

corresponding activity to successfully meet that lesson's learning objective(s) (i.e. Week 2 Lesson: Selecting a topic, Activity: Students will select a topic). As the semester progresses students will locate and evaluate the sources they will use for their annotated bibliography.

> **FIGURE 2.** Annotated Bibliography Assignment
>
> 1. Include a variety of 8 sources such as reference books, ebooks, print books, articles (magazine, journal, and newspaper), websites, and streaming videos.
> 2. Each annotation will include a summary of the source, your evaluation of the source using the CRAAP test (is the information reliable, is it a biased or objective resource, etc.) and a reflection on the source (how does this fit into your research, does it help you with your argument, has it changed your thinking on the subject?).
> 3. Each annotation should be between 100–300 words each.
> 4. The citations should be in MLA format.

In groups of 4, student sous chefs will collaborate to put together a well-rounded and delicious medley of sources (an annotated bibliography). Each student will locate at least 4 different types of sources (i.e. books, articles, websites, streaming media, etc.) and share the sources with their group members using the social bookmarking site Diigo. Students will evaluate each group member's sources for credibility, objectiveness, etc. (and tastiness). They will use Diigo's features to highlight, comment on, and annotate each source. In their groups, students will choose the best 8 sources they will use for their final annotated bibliography.

ALLERGY WARNINGS

Cook low and slow! Be sure students are working on their projects throughout the semester. Turn that oven light on and check in regularly!

CHEFS' NOTE

It is best to have them learn how to evaluate and cite sources in the beginning because they will need to evaluate and cite as they are finding their sources and building their annotated bibliography.

This lesson is beneficial for students in that it helps them build community and learn from each other, and it helps them to learn personal accountability and communication skills. It also teaches them how to use a valuable research tool.

ADDITIONAL RESOURCES

*   Diigo www.diigo.com

The Research Process Tasting Menu:
Bite-sized Information Literacy Skills Embedded in Online Courses

Jennifer C. Hill, Distance Education Librarian/Electronic Resources Manager, The Sheridan Libraries, Johns Hopkins University, jennifer.hill@jhu.edu

NUTRITION INFORMATION

The goal for this collaboration was to embed chunked information literacy skills throughout an entire online course. Working with one of our online partners, we embedded learning objects in two introductory-level courses: one is a general research course and the other is a subject-specific military course. The information literacy skills that we sprinkled throughout the courses built upon one another and ultimately lead students to writing their final papers.

SERVES

Serving size varies on enrollment in the online course at any given time.

COOKING TIME

About one month, but dependent on course launch timeframe; Additional time needed for updates to activities as necessary.

INGREDIENTS AND EQUIPMENT

- An enthusiastic librarian(s)
- Strong relationships with course developers/faculty
- A course that would benefit from information literacy skills (basically any course!)

PREPARATION

- Target a faculty member that you either have a good relationship with, or who has a course that they are developing/revising, or both! You just need to find *one* course.
- Convince him/her why their course would benefit from scaffolding information literacy instruction at point of need; i.e., students will demonstrate authentic learning and their final papers will be better!

- Ask what the final course outcome is (research paper, project, portfolio, etc.)
- Get familiar with the ACRL "Information Literacy Competency Standards."

COOKING METHOD

Once you know what the final course outcome is, work backwards. What are the different components of that whole meal that would need to be prepared and in what order? For example, if the final product is creating a research paper, create activities that work towards that goal.

Use a standard template for your instructional resources. Include your library branding, contact information, standard section headers, etc. You can include this same branding in PDFs as well as in video tutorials, such as Captivate files. Once they get familiar with the library's branding and template layout they will start to recognize the

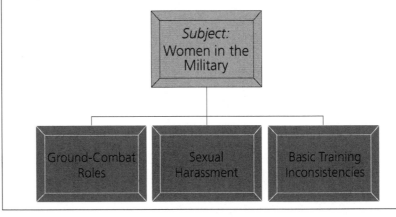

FIGURE 1. Excerpt from Activity #1: Choosing a Topic

2. After you have chosen a subject, think of ideas that you may want to write about that relate to your subject. You can use a mind mapping tool (in the Organizing Thoughts section), such as Bubbl.us to visually brainstorm keywords and phrases or you can simply use paper and pencil or anything else you are comfortable with. For example:

Subject: Women in the Military

Ground-Combat Roles

Sexual Harassment

Basic Training Inconsistencies

library activities and will be able to anticipate the flow.

For both of these courses, the final outcome was a research paper, so I embedded five activities throughout the course to work up to that result:

- Choosing a Topic
- Writing a Thesis Statement & Brainstorming
- Searching for Sources
- Evaluating Information & Organizing Your Ideas
- Avoiding Plagiarism & Citing Sources

Created 5 embedded activities. Each activity:
- Used our PDF library-branded template
- Fit on a 1–2 page document (not lengthy)
- Listed 2–3 learning outcomes
- Included a link to a short reading and/or video lesson
- Illustrated a step by step activity using a combination of text and graphics
- Was targeted to the particular population. In one case that included military students, so the topics, searches, resources, etc. were military-focused.
- Had a task to submit for assessment by instructor
- Was graded by the instructor with a rubric that was developed collaboratively

FIGURE 2. Research Activity #3: Snapshot: Search for Sources

Searching for Sources:
Research Activity #3

Now that you have chosen a topic, written a thesis statement, and brainstormed search words, you will now find resources for your final research paper.

Outcomes:
By the end of this activity you will be able to:
- Construct and implement effective search strategies
- Assess the quantity, quality, and relevance of the search results to determine whether alternative strategies or research databases should be used

Background:
The Library subscribes to many different research databases on your behalf. These databases contain all sorts of information—journal articles, online books, newspapers, reports, etc. A quick (Google-like) way to start your research is to use our **OneSearch** tool. OneSearch searches most of the research databases available in the Library at the same time! In the following activity you will use OneSearch to find at least five resources (articles, books, etc.) on your topic.

Two "Readings:"
- OneSearch Tips- Watch this short video to learn how to use OneSearch to find resources on your topic for your paper. You will learn how to do both a basic and advanced search using this tool.

- Search Tips & Tricks- Check out this 1-page tip sheet for handy search strategies that can be used in all databases, including OneSearch. (You may want to save it for future use)

ALLERGY WARNINGS
Collaborate with the faculty member so that they will be responsible for grading the activities. We worked with this instructor to develop a grading rubric that she could use to easily give credit. (You may need to train the instructor on some information literacy concepts as well). This makes embedding scalable.

In addition, use a format for your instructional resources that you can easily update. As times/collections change, you'll need to be able to tweak your embedded materials. We used PDFs that we linked in the course from our library's server. So, we could update the PDFs on the server and the version in the course would automatically change. Or if this is not possible, keep a spreadsheet of what you have in courses and review it at scheduled intervals.

CHEF'S NOTE

The students are responding well to the activities! Some of them have been calling the library for additional assistance and we work one-on-one with those students. Plus, it was a great idea to have the faculty member be responsible for grading the activities. Not only does this make embedding more scalable, but the faculty member can gauge each student's abilities in real time, prior to them submitting their final papers and can offer remedial help as needed or recommend them to contact the library. The library's contact information is included in the footer of each activity template for expert assistance at point of need. The initial project began with one general research course and then we were able to translate some of the same readings and activities to a subject-specific military course. Once we had a base of activities, we could tweak them to fit with this different population. In the future, these activities can continue to be modified for use in other courses. So, start stocking your pantry and then remix!

ADDITIONAL RESOURCES

*   https://bubbl.us/

Information Literacy MREs:
Pre-packaged Modules for Research Ease

Jennifer Kelley, Associate Professor and Reference Librarian, College of DuPage, kelleyj@cod.edu

NUTRITION INFORMATION

An information literacy module for research ease (MRE):

- Is easy to assemble using ingredients you probably already have on hand.
- Can be easily transported into any Learning Management System (LMS) package.
- Travels well for students on-the-go.
- Helps students and teaching faculty meet the recommended daily allowance of information literacy outcomes.

SERVES

Unlimited. This recipe can serve a single class or can be used as remediation for individual students.

COOKING TIME

Can be used for a quick weekday meal, or simmered over a semester.

INGREDIENTS AND EQUIPMENT

- Information literacy tutorial, either home-grown or imported (preferably Creative Commons-licensed)
- LMS

PREPARATION

Before assembling your Information Literacy MRE:

- Identify an information literacy (IL) tutorial that best meets your needs. If you are using an outside tutorial, does it meet your IL program outcomes? Does it meet your institutional outcomes? Are there areas that are not covered? Can you customize it to fit your needs?
- Consider assessment options. Does the tutorial have an assessment? Do you have an IL assessment tool that you can repurpose? Are there existing IL assessments you can adapt for your needs?

COOKING METHOD

Simply combine a web-based IL tutorial, an assessment and a set of outcomes, package them together in an LMS-ready module and serve it up to faculty—you've got instant, embeddable information MREs that any instructor can use, incorporate and adapt for students in any discipline, on-campus, online or at a distance.

The embedding process will vary depending on your institution's LMS. As Blackboard users, we were able to prepare the MREs in a development course shell, export the

FIGURE 1. Top level view of a unit in a blackboard course

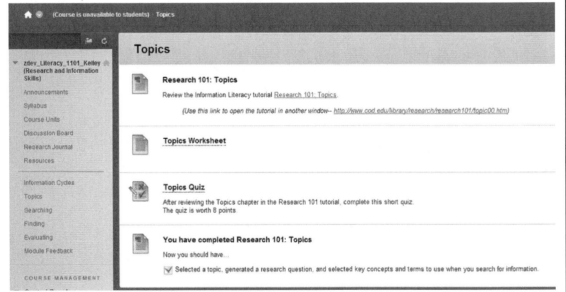

finished dish in a tidy zip file to-go box, and make it available for instructors to upload into their courses by using Dropbox as our delivery service. (See http://codlrc.org/IL/modules/start for our step-by-step instructions.)

Many pre-packaged tutorials come with their own set of outcomes, but if you'd like to whip up your own satisfying outcomes here are some thoughts:

- Consider what skills you'd like a student to have learned upon completion of each unit.
- Align those skills with your library's IL outcomes, your institution's IL outcomes, or ACRL's "Information Literacy Competency Standards for Higher Education."
- Every hour of content should only have about 2–3 outcomes—remember, you're teaching skills, not stuffing a turkey!

ALLERGY WARNINGS

Widespread adoption of MREs could result in overexposure. Students, fed a repeated diet of MREs semester-to-semester, while healthy and information literate, may become lethargic, peevish and annoyed with librarians.

CHEF'S NOTE

The College of DuPage Library has been packaging and distributing MREs in the form of our IL modules for over two years. The modules have been widely adopted by our English faculty who use them in ENGL 1101

FIGURE 2. Example of a Page within a Unit

Records

> **Records**
> Records are the building blocks of databases—they describe information sources.
> *Examples:*
> • Your driver's license is a record describing certain characteristics of the you.
> • An entry for Moby Dick in the Library's catalog is a record describing certain characteristics of the book.

It is unrealistic, at this time, to expect all information sources to come directly to a computer screen on demand. The reasons for this will be clearer to you as you become more experienced finding and using information.

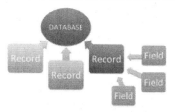

In the meantime, having a record describing a source that you can then find using your own abilities and knowledge is an excellent starting point. The description in a record uses elements called metadata [information about information]. In many cases, the text itself will have to be located using other finding tools. Some libraries provide links to the text of articles, when available, at their own expense.

> **Fields**
> Fields are the building blocks of records—they are the sections of a record where information is stored.
> *Examples:*
> • Your driver's license has fields for information like Name, Eye Color, Height, Address, etc.
> • The entry for Moby Dick has fields for Author, Title, Subject, Publisher, and Publication Date.

and 1102 courses—both face-to-face and online. Student feedback, gathered using a Google form that is uploaded into the course along with the modules, has been largely positive with a fair amount of enthusiasm thrown into the mix now and again as well:

- "Very helpful. I think every student should go through [them] once."
- "I think this was very good information. I learned new things that I will be using in writing my research paper."
- "I think that the tutorials introduced me to an extremely better method of researching than I have ever had before (if any) and it covered topics and techniques very well!"
- "This was a very good way for me to learn about researching and finding valuable sources for my papers."

Semester-to-semester, 70% of students report being only moderately familiar, somewhat familiar or not familiar at all with the concepts covered in the tutorials prior to using the modules. A slightly higher percentage reported finding the concepts covered in the tutorials useful.

ADDITIONAL RESOURCES

- Adebonojo, Leslie G. "A Way to Reach All of Your Students: The Course Management System." *Journal of Library & Information Services in Distance Learn-*

FIGURE 3. Summary of Responses Collected in Google Docs Survey

Summary See complete responses

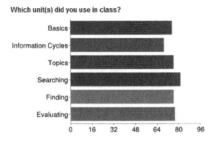

Which unit(s) did you use in class?

Basics	75	83%
Information Cycles	69	77%
Topics	76	84%
Searching	81	90%
Finding	76	84%
Evaluating	77	86%

People may select more than one checkbox, so percentages may add up to more than 100%.

Before using the tutorials, how familiar were you with the concepts covered in them?

1 - Very familiar	14	16%
2	29	32%
3	32	36%
4	12	13%
5 - Not familiar at all	3	3%

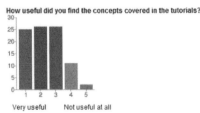

How useful did you find the concepts covered in the tutorials?

1 - Very useful	25	28%
2	26	29%
3	26	29%
4	11	12%
5 - Not useful at all	2	2%

ing 5, no. 105–113 (2011). doi:10.1080./153329 0X.2011.605936

- Flatley, Robert and Wiliam Jefferson. "Customizing and Using a Popular Online Information Literacy Tutorial: One Library's Experience." *Library Philosophy and Practice* 8, no. 2 (2006).
- Kelley, Jennifer. "Off the Shelf and Out of the Box: Saving Time, Meeting Outcomes and Reaching Students with Information Literacy Modules." *Journal of Library & Information Services in Distance Learning* 6, no. 3–4 (2012): 335–349.

FIGURE 4. View of Student Comments Collected in Google Docs Survey

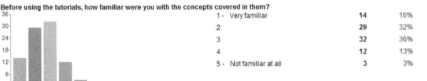

What topics, if any, would you like to see covered in an Information Literacy tutorial?	Comments?	For what class did you complete the tutorials?
	I loved the interactive pictures that were included in some of the tutorials. The quiz questions were relevant to the material learned. My favorite questions were the ones where we had to identify where the cited source came from.	English 1102
All were covered perfectly!	Very good job with the tutorial. Very informative!	English classes,Econ
	Very simple and easy to understand.	ECON 2201
I think everything necessary is covered.	Was easy to follow and useful.	Economics 2201
More about economics	very useful	Econo 2201
	Great review, always eager to learn how to improve my research.	Econ 2201
Primary and secondary resources	it was very helpful for my research paper.	Econo 2202
	Consider including an audio element to the module.	Macroeconomics

6. Tailgating: Embedding Outside of the Library and Outside of the Classroom

The recipes included in this section reflect the innovation of librarians in transforming their service models to meet students where they are. These librarians teach information literacy while preparing food in the dormitories, supporting art in the community, facilitating service learning projects, and more. The ideas presented here will push you out of your comfort zone and provide concrete steps for connecting with patrons outside traditional library walls.

Art and Soul:
Appetizers Designed for Community-based Working Artists

Judy Wanner, Associate Librarian, University of Guelph, jwanner@uoguelph.ca; Linda Graburn, Associate Librarian, University of Guelph, lgraburn@uoguelph.ca; Jane Burpee, Associate Librarian, University of Guelph, jburpee@uoguelph.ca

NUTRITION INFORMATION

Engaging the local arts community with the academic library is a wonderful way to develop partnerships with local working artists. Providing a building tour and hands-on instruction with electronic resources increases awareness of high quality library resources available to them. Next steps include designing future outreach opportunities that are specifically tailored to meet the specialized information needs of community-based artists working in different mediums. Longer-term goals include deeper embedding and cross pollination of understanding between the two communities.

COOKING TIME

Plan and assemble over 6–8 weeks.

INGREDIENTS AND EQUIPMENT

- Cooks with a taste for the arts and engagement, a hungry local arts community and a fabulous library collection:
  » Cook 1. The information literacy librarian
  » Cook 2. The information resources librarian
  » Cook 3. The scholarly communication librarian

- Desire to provide community artists with new sources that will both inspire and inform; the library's art collection, the archives collection, the book collection, a wide variety of electronic resources; a display of book titles related to relevant call number ranges and handouts to support future self-directed learning opportunities.

PREPARATION

FIGURE 1. Invitation to a community artist show

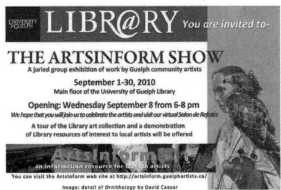

Use local contacts, including local art galleries, organizers of art festivals, art supply stores and the regional Arts Society to determine potential artists to personally invite. Include a survey of the individual artists and potential attendees to determine

how best to meet local needs. Design flyers with event details and contact information to leave with these local businesses to increase awareness of event. The ratio of attendees to instructors will dictate how many artists can be accommodated, during the hands-on training session and limit availability. Provide free campus parking to attendees. Offer a time for refreshments to provide attendees an opportunity to meet new colleagues and time to check out the book display arranged by Library of Congress (LC) subclasses.

COOKING METHOD

Explore the possible variations in information needs of the attendees and consider all potential collections, services and other resources that might be included in the orientation session. Be sure to consider non-traditional sources like Journal of Visualized Experiments (JoVE), an indexed medical science video library, or unique primary sources found in your archives collection, such as historical journals or personal letters, photos, posters, or a cookbook or theatre collection. Don't forget to provide the artists with a sense of the broad variety of resources available to them.

Offer a building tour to focus on the library as a place. This will provide opportunity to showcase your library's art collection as well as time to see scholarly sources that inspire the process of creativity and the development of new knowledge. Create handouts that include information on community borrowing privileges, building hours, academic schedule and campus parking, building maps, descriptions of specialized collections held in archives and a breakdown of relevant LC classes, to facilitate future visits to browse the circulating collection.

Offer hands-on instruction and provide an overview of the library's web pages, catalogue and e-resources. Printing, copying and downloading options as well as wireless access should also be covered.

Seek input on how well expectations were met. Gather ideas for future sessions and suggestions on how to improve the session. Don't forget contact information to encourage individuals interested in meeting one to one with a librarian at a later date.

ALLERGY WARNINGS
Ensure that you **take time to gain buy-in from administration**. They need to see value and the benefits and opportunities in developing engagement with the artist community. This may be a low priority for your administration. Expect push back. If you can't stand the heat, get out of the kitchen.

Community First. Ensure that you take time to **understand the interests and needs of the artists** in your community. There is a distinct difference between supporting campus fine arts students vs. working artists. Community artists may not recognize the importance and significance of the resources available to them in the academic library for their creative process.

FIGURE 2. Community artist and retired librarian Pat Eaves Brown

Ask the community what it wants. Being able to develop a service that is relevant to their needs is a challenge…we recommend a survey of the artists as a way to understand their interests and needs. This will help you to tailor the session.

- Planning an event takes **time**. Community engagement may not be seen as a regular part of your workload. Time available for your service activities may be sparse. Members of the planning committee may not be able to devote more than a few hours each per week on planning activities.
- Be sure to find ways to **reach out and promote** your event to a wide network of artists in your community. Initially, locating and getting the word out to the community artists may prove to be a challenge. Working with established artist collectives and local associations is recommended.
- Ensure that you take the time to **deepen your understanding of all the various resources** and services available in your library that the artists in your community are able to access.
- Don't forget to **assess your success**. It is important to evaluate the impact of this community engagement.

CHEF'S NOTE
By embedding with our off-campus communities we spread the word about the variety of information and resources available at the library. The skills development and awareness within the artists to inspire their creativity will be invaluable to them.

The session is a starting point for developing relationships. This is really about relationship building activity that can support broader engagement initiatives. There is potential for the reciprocity of the relationship to extend to other campus stakeholder groups.

The experience will allow librarians to look at what the academic library has to offer from a different lens. Perspectives will be nurtured by meeting a group of professional artists. Activities will meet a need that no one else is meeting.

Activities will expand the definition of community and access demonstrating that our academic library is truly open to our community.

VARIATIONS

This recipe can be successfully tailored for any type of community group: writers, musicians, chefs, and environmental activists.

Blend librarian skills, library resources, and serve your community.

ADDITIONAL RESOURCES

- "Information Literacy in Art." Association of College and Research Libraries. Accessed June 18, 2013. http://wikis.ala.org/acrl/index.php/Information_Literacy_in_Art
- Journal of Visualized Experiments (JoVE) http://www.jove.com/

- Directions for cooking up a survey may be found in: Eaves-Brown, Patricia, Judith Wanner, and Linda Graburn. "Beyond the Ivied Walls: Outreach to the Art Community." In *The Handbook of Art and Design Librarianship*, edited by Amanda Gluibizzi and Paul Glassman. 229–243. New York, N.Y.: Facet Publishing, 2010.

Memes on the Menu:
Tasty Tactics to Get your Athletes on Track

Nicole Pagowsky, Instructional Services Librarian, University of Arizona, pagowskyn@u.library.arizona.edu; Erica DeFrain, Assistant Library Professor, University of Vermont, edefrain@uvm.edu

NUTRITION INFORMATION
This recipe introduces and reinforces information literacy and critical thinking skills in a fun and engaging way for our student athletes.

COOKING TIME
Three 30-minute workshops throughout the sports' season (Fall for football, Spring for basketball and baseball).

ACRL INFORMATION DIETARY STANDARDS ADDRESSED
ACRL Visual Literacy standards: 3, 4

INGREDIENTS AND EQUIPMENT
- Computer lab with projector
- CRAAP test
- Meme worksheet

PREPARATION
Work with athletic tutors to determine when students have upcoming research assignments and downtime between games. We have developed a series of three fun, fast-paced workshops—introducing database searching, critical evaluation, and plagiarism—that are meant to supplement other instruction athletes are receiving so they are building skills and getting addi-

tional support. We also offer one workshop per academic year to tutors and academic advisors to refresh their skills and knowledge of the Libraries. Since different sports are in season in different semesters, we provide workshops to high profile athletes who might encounter the most difficulty with student success due to more regimented scheduling; in the fall, we work with football, and in the spring, basketball and baseball.

To prepare for the activity, librarians select 2–3 (inoffensive) memes that are currently popular (see Figure 1).

The clearest definition of a meme actually comes from Wikipedia[1], explaining that a meme originates from "imitation," where an "idea, behavior, or style" is replicated within a particular culture. Typically memes are expressed in a humorous way reflecting on a current event, cultural norm, or even a recent faux pas on the Internet.

FIGURE 1. Cat memes are very popular.

- Find ones that are clear with recognizable images, since students will need a basis to think of their research keywords. Students will employ visual literacy skills to understand the context of these images, since memes are both images and text. There is plenty of room for creativity to understand what these memes are implying, and students can do research on any aspect of what they see in the meme.

COOKING METHOD

1. Use this tasty technique to wrap-up another successful sports season
2. *Hors d'oeuvres*: Heat up the class with a 10 minute research refresher covering library databases, CRAAP test evaluation, and citing sources.
3. *Mise en place*: Prep your sous chefs to take control by forming teams of 3–4 students, handing out materials, going over the rules, and completing a **meme worksheet** together (5–10 minutes).

The students become the master chefs: Let the games begin as the teams compete to fill out the worksheet first. Teams must present their findings to the class for approval. The taste of victory is sweetened with candy bars for winners.

ALLERGY WARNINGS

Don't choose memes that could offend a broad audience of students' palettes!

CHEFS' NOTE

The activity: Because many millennials are interested and involved in Internet culture, we wanted to tie library research and critical thinking to something they would be familiar with: memes. Instead of having students come up with a topic, which can be difficult and stressful, we wanted them to get comfortable with research first. Using graphical memes forces students to come up with a question based on something they are curious about: what does this mean, and what does it mean within culture? Research typically works with an individual finding a gap in the literature and having a question, so we wanted to model this as much as possible. This also would deter students from solely summarizing, which can often lead to plagiarism.

Initially allowing students to use mostly Internet resources made it easier for them to explain the meme, but they struggled more in assessing credibility. Also, in assigning different memes to each team, some were more complicated for students to research than others, so this gave an unfair advantage to certain groups. Choosing only memes with cultural or historical significance that would have more content available when researching can help with this issue. Another concern was students simply locating pieces of information on the site they chose to evaluate and then regurgitating this on their worksheet, rather than using critical thinking skills to examine credibility. It's good to remind students to think critically about what they're finding: instead of just writing down the year of publication or author name, think about if having more recent information on the topic is essential, or the affiliations and expertise of the author.

The students: Within the general student population, University of Arizona football players are of particular concern when it comes to student retention: with a 53 percent Athletic Graduation Success Rate, the UA is in second-to-last place among Pac-12 schools.[2] This, combined with the Arizona Board of Regents' high interest in improving student retention, makes it essential for the University of Arizona Libraries to support athletics and related programs. With retention being a major concern both locally and nationally, embedding in non-disciplinary units while supporting University learning objectives demonstrates the Libraries' value and connection to campus.

Because these students' schedules are so packed and pre-determined for them, it can be difficult to hold their attention when they have a lot of other work to complete, and likely many other things on their mind. Keeping the session short and to the point for them helps, as does making the activity engaging, while relating directly to their assignments (if possible).

The department: Developing close relationships with athletics' tutors and academic advisors keeps us abreast of any upcoming assignments and commitments the athletes have so that we can schedule workshops accordingly. In conjunction with student instruction, we also offer training for specialists working with the athletes, taking a "train-the-trainer" approach for scalability. We are then able to impart library information and research skills to the students through the tutors.

To keep collaboration going and to assess information literacy sessions, we ask both students and tutors to fill out a short survey to measure student success. By comparing Fall and Spring semester responses, we can see how students have progressed over the semester, and we also see the difference in help requested from the tutors over the course of the semester to get a holistic evaluation of our efforts.

NOTES

1. "Meme," *Wikipedia*, Accessed May 29, 2013, http://en.wikipedia.org/wiki/Meme.
2. Patrick Finley, "Academics: Graduation Rates on Upswing for Cats," *Arizona Daily Star*, October 26, 2012, http://azstarnet.com/sports/college/wildcats/academics-graduation-rates-on-upswing-for-cats/article_98c49c1b-d40d-5044-988a-78082cf1c58e.html

ADDITIONAL RESOURCES

- "Evaluating Information: Applying the CRAAP Test." Meriam Library, California State University, Chico, CA. Accessed May 29, 2013. http://www.csuchico.edu/lins/handouts/eval_websites.pdf.
- "Know Your Meme." *Internet Meme Database*. Accessed May 29, 2013. http://knowyourmeme.com/.
- "Meme Generator." *Meme Generator*. Accessed May 29, 2013. http://memegenerator.net/.
- "Make & Share Your Meme." *Quickmeme*. Accessed May 29, 2013. http://www.quickmeme.com/
- Pagowsky, Nicole and Erica DeFrain. "Evaluating Websites Activity" (Handout for classroom activity, May 29, 2013). http://nicolepagowsky.info/documents/memeworksheet2012.pdf.

Resources on engaging student athletes:

- Forys, Marsha, John Forys, Ann Ford, and Jeff Dodd. "Information Literacy Program for Student Athletes at the University of Iowa." *Research Strategies* 17, no. 4 (January 1, 2000): 353–58.
- Pagowsky, Nicole, and Jaime Hammond. "A Programmatic Approach Systematically Tying the Library to Student Retention Efforts on Campus." *College and Research Libraries News* 73, no. 10 (November 1, 2012): 582.
- Puffer-Rothenberg, Maureen, and Susan E. Thomas. "Providing Library Outreach to Student Athletes." *The Reference Librarian* 32 (February 1, 2000): 131–146.

FIGURE 2. Survey to measure student success

Survey Examples
Assessment for student athletes:
1. What did you find most useful from the librarian visits during the semester to help you in your coursework?

2. What library service or resource do you think will be the most helpful to you as a student?

3. What other topic(s) would you want covered in library presentations?

Assessment for staff:
1. How would you describe the overall quality of this semester's workshops? Poor Fair Good Very Good Excellent

2. Please circle which option best represents how you feel about the following statement: My students have demonstrated an improvement in their research skills because of these workshops Strongly Disagree, Disagree, I don't know, Agree, Strongly Agree

3. Please explain your answer to the previous question:

4. What do you find to be the most common problem(s) athletes have with library research?

5. What library research skill(s) do you think would be most useful for athletes to build as students?

Whipping up a Better World:
Embedding Library Instruction into Service Learning Classes with Community Based Research Assignments

Theresa McDevitt, PhD, Outreach Librarian, Stapleton Library, Indiana University of Pennsylvania Libraries, mcdevitt@iup.edu

NUTRITION INFORMATION
This project introduces and reinforces best practices in finding, evaluating, and ethically using information by employing students to do a real life research project for a community partner.

SERVES
Up to 30, although the number of students will be limited by the number of community partners available.

COOKING TIME
One semester.

INGREDIENTS AND EQUIPMENT
- Classroom for instruction with an overhead projector and access to the Internet
- Computer lab where students have access to the Internet and library databases, or ask students to bring their own devices
- Research projects provided by community partners
- Subject discipline faculty who seek authentic assignments to engage students, develop their interest in community involvement, and provide them with resume-building real life work experiences.

PREPARATION
- Connect with an instructor for a class in any discipline that asks students to do research as part of their course requirements. The ideal class to work with is one that already includes a community-based research project. However, this instruction can be embedded in courses in any discipline where professors want to provide authentic, problem-based research assignments to students instead of the traditional research paper.

FIGURE 1. Information literacy game prepared with library as community partner

- Discuss the educational and societal benefits of service learning experiences with instructors.
- Locate community organizations that could benefit from a research project performed by student researchers. (Some partners that we worked with included the YMCA, the Girl Scouts, a local domestic violence shelter, the community garden, and even our library and our local public library. Offices of Service Learning can assist tremendously with this or ask students to visit community involvement fairs).
- Work with instructor to design a research based service learning assignment that will benefit the community partner and fulfill student class requirements
- Assist instructor in designing a rubric for evaluation of the final projects that includes requiring quality sources, standard citation, and ethical use of information sources to get a good grade.

COOKING METHOD
The librarian can attend all of the class sessions or only those where information literacy skills are being introduced or practiced.

Sessions should include:

1. To begin, community partners should be invited to a class session to tell students what they do and what their research project was and how it would help them. The students should be required to select a partner before they begin doing any research work and information literacy instruction sessions begin.

2. Once students have decided upon their community partners and what their research projects will be, either individually or as a group, they should begin their research using their chosen research project topics. The librarian should provide an introduction to finding the best sources with the greatest efficiency. In this session, the librarian should introduce best practices in finding information through library databases and Internet sites. Topics covered should include: How to efficiently and effectively search databases, how they compare with information found freely on the Internet, what the invisible web is, and why students benefit from learning how to search them and by using the information found there. Students should be given time to do their own searching and an assignment requiring them to find some relevant sources on their chosen research topics.

3. When students have collected some sources, the librarian should provide a session to assist students to develop skills in evaluating resources. It takes a bit longer, but sessions where students

are able to brainstorm their own evaluation criteria for both web sources and tangible resources are probably more effective than simply providing a rubric for evaluation. Again, either individually or in groups, students should work with the resources they have found and choose those that are the most relevant and of the highest quality. Having them work in groups to compare resources is particularly effective.

FIGURE 2. Internet Evaluation and Citation Worksheet

> ## Internet Evaluation and Citation Worksheet
>
> Name_____
>
> Write the correct APA Citation for the website that you brought to class today.
>
> Write an annotation for it in the space below. Remember that annotations should be at least two sentences long and include information on as many as possible of the following: Relevancy, Authority, Accuracy, Currency, and Documentation.
>
> Now find a partner. Compare the websites you brought to class today. Discuss your annotations and your decisions about each site's relevancy, authority, accuracy, currency, and documentation. Choose one of the sites as the highest quality and the best suited to the research needs of your community partner. Write the name of the site below and discuss why it is best in the space below.

4. When students have decided what sources they are going to use, the librarian should do a session assisting them to develop skills in citing them

in standard bibliographic styles. This can be done in a variety of ways from working with style guides or teaching citation tools such as EndNote, RefWorks or freely available tools such as Zotero (which allows for collaboration for students doing group work) or Easybib. Students should be cautioned the bibliographic management tools are not substitutes for knowing how to cite things correctly. They are great tools but they sometimes make errors that must be corrected.

5. A session on using information ethically should also be included. In class or out of class readings, a lecture, or film should introduce basic information on plagiarism and copyright. This should be followed by interactive discussion created by posing scenarios that students should respond to. This can be done with Clickers and Poll Everywhere as well.

6. Librarians could lead or assist in class sessions where students work on their projects and help them hone the skills introduced in earlier sessions.

7. Librarians could lead or assist in peer review sessions where students review each others' projects and provide assistance with any information literacy-related issues that arise.

8. Librarians should attend sessions where students present their research findings/projects and to reflect upon their experience with doing the research and gaining information literacy skills, either in writing or publicly.

ALLERGY WARNINGS

Working with real life projects is sometimes challenging and unpredictable. It is not unusual for community organizations' internal issues to prevent them from continuing to work with students for the entire semester. It is best if the partners work closely with the instructor as an intermediary. If visits to the community partner's organization are required, transportation issues, or waivers of accidental injury might arise.

CHEF'S NOTE

Not all students will be engaged by the real world challenge of service learning. Because you are working with a real life organization the outcomes are uncertain but the potential for transformational experiences and resume-building opportunities far outweigh any negative aspects.

Student reflection is almost always positive. They see it as a good use of their time, they like it when group work is permitted, they feel the experience is rewarding, and often get something to add to their vitae.

This type of assignment requires more work for the faculty member, but will appeal to professors who find that their students are not engaged by traditional research paper assignments, have social justice interests, want to make class work more meaningful and to help students build real life researching skills. Try connecting with instructors after service learning or teaching practice workshops to find good prospects. People at such workshops tend to be motivated in this. You can also assure instructors that, while it is more work, it is worth the extra effort to promote good causes and, with the librarians help, it isn't that much more work.

ADDITIONAL RESOURCES

- Barry, Maureen. "Research for the Greater Good: Incorporating Service Learning in an Information Literacy Course at Wright State University." *College & Research Libraries News* 72, no. 6 (2011): 345–348.
- Herther, Nancy. K. "Service Learning and Engagement in the Academic Library: Operating Out of the Box." *College & Research Libraries News* 69, no. 7 (2008): 386–389.
- Meyer, Nadean J. and Ielleen R. Miller. "The Library as Service-Learning Partner: A Win–Win Collaboration with Students and Faculty." *College & Undergraduate Libraries* 15, no. 4 (2008): 399–413.
- Riddle, John S. "Where's the Library in Service Learning?: Models for Engaged Library Instruction." *The Journal of Academic librarianship* 29, no. 2 (2003): 71–81.

Taking the Research Game on the Road:
Librarian's Office Hours for Student Athletes

Susan Avery, Instructional Services Librarian and Associate Professor, Undergraduate Library, University of Illinois at Urbana-Champaign, skavery@illinois.edu

NUTRITION INFORMATION

Gaining a better understanding of the student athlete is the first step in providing services to this population. As college students, student athletes face particularly unique challenges that can impact their ability to take advantage of traditional library services and workshops geared toward the typical undergraduate. A librarian's office hours are the ideal hybrid of reference and instruction, meeting students at their point of need and providing librarians the opportunity to take advantage of valuable teachable moments they provide. Adapting a librarian's office hours for student athletes is a great way to connect with and serve this unique student population.

While it is true that student athletes are often isolated from the rest of the student body due to the time demands placed on them, they maintain the same needs for services as other students. In addition to being full-time students, athletes have significant commitments to their sport and their schedules tend to be extremely regimented in order to fit in classes and practice time. The addition of games, matches, and grueling travel schedules when their sport is in session increases the challenges they face. Jolly (2008) observes student athletes tend to: be tightly scheduled and regiment-ed, feel isolated from other students and campus academic life, be less likely to seek help than non-athletes, and sometimes feel discriminated against by faculty.[1] Harmon concurs with Jolly and observes athletes of color have particular difficulties academically. She emphasizes the importance of "examining our perceptions of student athletes and athletics, educating ourselves about the student athlete experience, and finding ways to collaborate in meaningful ways with athletics staff…"[2] Providing library services that meet the needs of student athletes serves to connect them to the library and enhance their academic success.

The National Collegiate Athletic Association (NCAA) has implemented a number of metrics for member institutions in order to gauge the academic progress of student athletes, both individually and by sport. For example, Division I institutions are expected to demonstrate that student athletes are maintaining academic progress through an Academic Progress Rate (APR) and a Graduation Success Rate (GSR). Students at Division II institutions are expected to demonstrate an Academic Success Rate. These NCAA policies are intended to hold institutions accountable for the performance of student athletes in the classroom and failure to maintain adequate rates can impact both practice time and scholarship availability.

Ultimately, academic success of student athletes is the responsibility of each institution and providing support services at individual institutions can be instrumental to this success. Partnering with an athletic department in the provision of library services is not only an advantage to student athletes, it is also an example of a positive outreach and public relations endeavor on the part of the library.

COOKING TIME

The service is intended to meet the needs of student athletes when they are actively engaged in the research process. Use your library's reference statistics to determine which weeks are the busiest and schedule accordingly. A starting guideline would be to offer the service six to eight weeks each semester. Limiting each session to two hours should be sufficient.

INGREDIENTS AND EQUIPMENT

- Academic support facility for student athletes OR library space
- A computer with access to the library's webpage and resources
- Copies of commonly used library guides and handouts

- A librarian eager to work with student athletes

PREPARATION

1. Identify and connect with academic support personnel in your university's athletic department. (The size of this office will be dependent on the size of your institution.) The people in this office will be well aware of the academic needs of student athletes and will be able to provide you with ideas for the best days, times, and locations for providing an office hours service.

2. Identify a person in the athlete's academic support office to serve as your primary liaison. This will be most helpful in facilitating the service, sharing the library's goals, and communicating with other academic counselors, tutors, and student athletes.

3. Learn what strategies academic support personnel have in place for communicating with student athletes and utilize these options. These may include weekly newsletters, text messages, tutoring sessions, and meetings in which to publicize and encourage use of the service. In addition, create flyers and table tents that advertise the service (including dates, time, location) to place in facilities used by student athletes and posters to display when librarian's office hours are taking place.

4. Consider creating a LibGuide or similar tool that can be used by athletes when they are on the road for away games or matches. This can serve as a one-stop point for athletes to connect with library resources, citation information, links to course information, and the library's chat reference service.

5. If the facility used by your student athletes provides computers, make sure access to the library is provided as a link on the main page or desktop.

COOKING METHOD

- Collaborate with your liaison in the academic support office to identify the best time and location for office hours.
- Upon arrival at your office hours location, place posters that indicate the service is in session at locations where the athletes will see them.
- To publicize your presence, announce the service is now available. This may require walking around the facility making numerous individual announcements or a general announcement on a public address system. Check with the facility you are working in to identify the preferred method.
- Be friendly and welcoming!

ALLERGY WARNINGS

Consistency in the time, place, and librarian providing the service are all important elements when establishing a new service, particularly one for a population that hasn't been served in this way prior. Having a familiar face in a familiar space at the same time each week is helpful in encouraging use of the service.

CHEF'S NOTE

Be prepared to assist your student athletes with questions from a variety of disciplines. It is likely more questions will focus on general first and second year courses and citation assistance. However, it is impossible to know in advance what kinds of questions students will have and what resources you will need to use. Think of this as a reference desk experience where you must be prepared for whatever questions come your way!

Success may not come immediately. As with any new service it may take several semesters to establish a success. Revisit the suggestions listed in the Preparations section periodically and maintain an ongoing relationship with your academic services liaison. Keep in mind there are many ways to measure success and the provision of such a service for student athletes can enhance a positive image of the library on your campus.

ADDITIONAL RESOURCES

- For more information about NCAA academic policies see: http://www.ncaa.org/wps/wcm/connect/public/ncaa/academics/index.html
- Noel Harmon. "Overscheduled and Overcommitted." *About Campus* 14 (2010): 26–29.
- Christopher J. Jolly. "Raising the Question #9: Is the Student-Athlete Population Unique? And Why Should We Care?" *Communication Education* 57 (2008): 145–151.

The Golden Carrot:
Cooking Demonstrations as Library Outreach

Mark Bieraugel, Business Librarian, California Polytechnic State University, mbieraug@calpoly.edu

NUTRITION INFORMATION

The purpose of this activity is to introduce students to librarians and to library services in a friendly and informal way by embedding the librarian in the student's residence hall. Outreach to students to introduce librarians and our services can be challenging without a compelling reason for students to show up. One approach is to work with existing programs that have previously been overlooked. My campus housing division offers "Cooking in the Canyon," in which a faculty member teaches a two hour cooking class to sophomores at their residence hall. This program is specifically for sophomores to connect them with the larger campus community and to make them more independent. The sophomore resident hall apartments include full kitchens. If you don't have a program in place you could try a cooking demonstration class at your library.

The sophomores targeted by this session generally have an awareness of the library, at least as a study space, but might not know about subject area librarians and the online resources we provide. This event helps to build awareness and to present the librarians as approachable and fun members of the campus community. Very few students come to office hours of librarians, so this is another method for librarians to connect with students where they are.

SERVES

25 students or fewer, although larger kitchens can accommodate more cooks.

COOKING TIME

Two hours or less depending on the dish or drink you're demonstrating.

INGREDIENTS AND EQUIPMENT

- An easy and simple dish or drink to prepare. Students love bread, cheese, and sweets
- Copies of recipe to hand out
- Enthusiastic librarian
- The necessary ingredients and cooking tools
- Business cards for subject area librarians or promotional materials
- Optional: life sized 'headshot/portraits' of all librarians on sticks to introduce other subject area librarians

PREPARATION

"Cooking in the Canyon" was created in 2008 to help teach students living in on-campus residence halls how to cook. Faculty and staff can volunteer to teach students how to prepare something to eat or drink. Part of my outreach efforts includes interacting with students outside of the classroom or library, connecting with them in fun ways. University housing has programming that they advertise, promote, and oversee, making for a built in way for librarians to readily interact with students.

Find a recipe for a suitable appetizer, dish, non-alcoholic drink, or dessert and practice making it. Print out recipe as handouts. Buy ingredients, and be sure to check with institution's purchasing department to see if you can order the ingredients in bulk. Students can share rolling pins, knives, and other implements, but it is helpful to have one implement for every three or four attendees. Optional—print out photos of subject librarians, apply to foam core, and put on sticks, such as wood paint mixers.

COOKING METHOD

Warm, welcoming, and fun are three important ingredients to making this activity successful. The goal is to introduce librarians in a low key way, and food is "the golden carrot" to lure students to the event. By joining students where they live, by doing a cooking demonstration, by making something and then having the students make it themselves, you're learning by doing in a fun, low stress way. This activity brings the librarian to the students, and students are more receptive during instruction sessions when they know the librarian. This activity connects the librarian to the student community with a fun activity.

Figure 1. Librarian chef Mark Bieraugel explains library services to students.

At the beginning of the demonstration introduce yourself, hold up the life size face placards of the other librarians as their introduction, and then quickly segue into the most important thing—the food. During the time the students are making their own dishes you can talk about a student's major, their classes, what types of projects they are working on. Key to the success of this event is going to the student's residence hall, so they don't need to go far to attend the event.

Figure 2. Students and librarian Mark Bieraugel sample recipes in the residence hall.

ALLERGY WARNINGS

Recipes requiring extensive and difficult knife work should not be demonstrated. What might be tasty to a middle-aged librarian might not be to a 19-year-old, so check with your student assistants and others to see if your dish is appetizing college-aged students. You might also consider vegetarian and gluten free options.

FIGURE 3. Assembling the finished recipe.

CHEF'S NOTE

The best dishes are those that the students assemble and then can immediately eat. For my first session I made puff pastry cheese straws that required baking. This meant the students returned to their own kitchens or to the public kitchen to bake their cheese straws. In my next cooking lesson I taught to make a huge variety of finger sandwiches, none of which required cooking, just assembling. This was a huge success and the students ate everything. For my latest demonstration I chose BBQ chicken sandwiches with a bunch of different toppings, which used rotisserie chickens, buns, and numerous toppings. Again, no cooking, just some assembly required.

Academic-focused outreach efforts to the same population yielded no attendees, while a food-focused activity two weeks later attracted twenty-two students. Food is "the golden carrot" to draw students to events.

ADDITIONAL RESOURCES
- "50 Tea Sandwiches." *Food Network.* Accessed June 3, 2013.
- http://www.foodnetwork.com/recipes-and-cooking/50-tea-sandwiches/index.html
- "Easy No-Cook Appetizer Recipes." *EatingWell.* Accessed June 3, 2013.
- http://www.eatingwell.com/recipes_menus/recipe_slide-shows/easy_no_cook_appetizer_recipes?slide=1#leaderboardad
- "Quick & Easy Recipes." *Epicurious.* Accessed June 3, 2013.
- http://www.epicurious.com/recipes-menus/quickeasy/recipes

Blending in Library Instruction is a Recipe for Academic Success:
Embedding Information Literacy Instruction in Campus Life

Theresa McDevitt, PhD, Outreach Librarian, Indiana University of Pennsylvania Libraries, mcdevitt@iup.edu

NUTRITION INFORMATION

This recipe will support student academic success by building their knowledge of how the library can help them and by improving their information literacy skills.

SERVES

Serves up to 30 chefs-in-training (residence hall student directors) or 10–20 residence hall residents.

COOKING TIME

One semester or school year.

INGREDIENTS AND EQUIPMENT

- Overhead projector and access to the Internet for some sessions
- Computer lab, or ask students to bring their own devices for some sessions
- Partnership with student life employees and/or staff in the housing office

PREPARATION

1. Meet with student life/housing staff to discuss shared goals of supporting student academic success.
2. Brainstorm ways that the library can embed instruction into pre-existing student life/housing initiatives.
3. Hold focus groups with residence hall student mentors to ask what programs

would be well received in halls or do other formal or informal feedback gathering to discover what students might be most interested in learning from library staff.

FIGURE 1. Handout detailing the Library Discovery Investigation/Presentation activity

Library Discovery Investigation/Presentation

IUP Indiana University of Pennsylvania

IUP LIBRARIES

For this challenge you will be asked to do three things: investigate, present, and rate your fellow students on their presentations.

1) **Investigation.** You will choose/be assigned a place or service in the Library. Some information will be provided to you, but it is your job to investigate the place or service by visiting the place or searching for information on our web page. You might also find information by talking to people at the service desks, or to other students who might be using the place or service (but don't bother people who are trying to study!). The object is to find enough information to tell your fellow students where it is, why it is useful, and why people like it when we do our tour.

2) **Presentation:** Next, we will travel through the Library and when we get to the place that you have selected, you will tell your fellow students about that place or service by answering the following questions:
a) What is the place?
b) How is it used, what can you do there?
c) Why it is useful to students including a real life example.

3) **Rating and Choosing a Winner:** When the tour is completed, we will gather in the classroom to vote on whose presentation was the most informative and entertaining. Those individuals will be awarded prizes.

COOKING METHOD

Procedures should vary based upon the information gathered during the meetings with student life/housing permanent and student employees but possibilities include:

1. Offer interactive train the trainer library orientations for residence hall student mentors which point out the library and student life's shared objectives in supporting student academic success and introducing the places, services and resources that would benefit students. Possible methods of engaging students include:

   a. Let the students be the guide with a library discovery orientation. Make a list of fifteen or so of the most important things and places in the library. Assign places to groups of attendees to investigate. Allow them time to investigate and then ask them to report what they found to their colleagues. Librarian adds missing information or gently corrects misinformation (This activity is based on "Library's Best Beach Ball Game.[1]")

   b. Use the Cephalonian Method to engage students during an orientation by supplying them with amusing, but relevant information-evoking questions which allow the librarian the opportunity to provide the same information he or she would anyway, with greater impact. An example of the questions would be, "I just slept through my 9:00 am class. Where can I copy my friend's notes?" (For more questions and more information, see Cephalonian Method history and description link below.)

c. Show engaging library videos as part of presentation. Include interviews with students working at service desks or of upper level students who will report successful use of the library.

2. Embed library tours, games, and challenges into beginning of the semester, Welcome Weekends, or other orientations planned to teach new students about university support services, and offer prizes to those who successfully complete challenges. Possibilities include:

a. Ask students to solve a library mystery/scavenger hunt (require exposure to significant library services, places and resources in order to solve the mystery)

b. Hold a library open house and ask students to visit a certain number of stations in order to qualify for prize drawing.

c. Host a library booth at student association/involvement fair. Take pictures of students in front of book-

shelf back drops and send them the photos via email. Film students talking about what they think about the library. Ask students to respond to a question about using the library to qualify for a drawing for library mugs or thumb drives.

3. Offer a series of programs in the residence halls:

a. Introduction to library services, resources and places similar to that offered during the train the trainer workshops. End with a library Jeopardy game and offer prizes to winners.

b. Citation and plagiarism awareness sessions including:
   » Citation style or Zotero, Easybib or other bibliographic management system workshop
   » Dropbox or other research support tools workshops.
   » Turnitin workshop
   » Plagiarism scenario workshop[2]
   » Offer workshop in finding the best resources for research. Such "Research Rescue" sessions might be offered at both the beginning and near the end of the semester. Begin session by asking students to bring projects that they are working on and work from there.

c. Instruction in evaluating resources. Discuss the potential value/hazards of research based solely on use of Wikipedia and other fluid, unreliable Internet resources.

d. Library resources to reduce stress, focus, and do well on finals. Introduce what the library can do to support students during the entire semester and point out any special program services that are offered during finals

ALLERGY WARNINGS

Residence hall student mentors and other employees are likely to be enthusiastic and happy for partners in improving students' academic success. Students living in the residence halls may be more reserved. Don't be discouraged if your programs don't draw more than a dozen students. Students who do attend will gain important skills which will help them to succeed, will be more likely to visit the library and seek assistance from library staff, and may encourage others to come as well and share the information they have gained with their peers.

Programs offered in conjunction with other events are generally best attended, so embedding sessions in other events is advised. Holding sessions in a well-traveled area, providing food, or offering incentives such as point systems, t-shirts, and contests may increase attendance.

CHEF'S NOTE

These programs have been quite successful on our campus in building strong relationships between students and librarians as well as improving students' information literacy skills. Librarians notice the same students who they meet in open houses and residence hall sessions are likely to contact them when they are in need of assistance and to come to the library. Librarians, too, learn about student needs and preferences from working with them in small groups. It is a win-win situation.

FIGURE 2. Graduate students in Student Affairs and Higher Education Allison Shumar and Amelia Shill pose with IUP mascot Norm and library stacks background during IUP Day, a student engagement event held annually at the beginning of the fall semester.

NOTES

1. McDevitt, Theresa and Rosalee Stilwell. "Library's Best Beach Ball Game." In *Let the games begin: Engaging students with field-tested interactive information literacy instruction,* edited by Theresa McDevitt, 23–27. New York: Neal-Schuman Publishers, 2011.

2. Ariew, Susan and Heather Runya. "Using Scenarios to Teach Undergraduates about Copyright, Fair Use, and Plagiarism." *LOEX 2006*, accessed June 3, 2013, http://commons.emich.edu/cgi/viewcontent.cgi?article=1027&context=loexconf2006

ADDITIONAL RESOURCES

*   Barnes, Newkerk and Gail Peyton. "Reaching Out to the Net Generation on Campus: Promoting the MSU Libraries in the Residence Halls." *Public Services Quarterly* 2, no. 4 (2006): 47–68.
*   Cummings, Laura Ursin. "Bursting out of the Box: Outreach to the Millennial Generation through Student Services Programs." *Reference Services Review*, 35, no. 2 (2007): 285–295.
*   Morgan, Nigel and Linda Davies. "Innovative Library Induction–Introducing the 'Cephalonian Method.'" *Sconul Focus* 32 (Summer/Autumn 2004): 4–8.
*   Morgan, Nigel. "The Official Cephalonian Method Page: Don't Just Present it… Ceph It!" Accessed June 3, 2013, http://www.cardiff.ac.uk/insrv/educationandtraining/infolit/cephalonian-method/index.html
*   Snyder Broussard, Mary Jane. "Secret Agents in the Library: Integrating Virtual and Physical Games in a Small Academic Library." *College & Undergraduate Libraries* 17, no 1 (2010): 20–30.
*   Strothmann, Molly and Karen Antelli. "The Live-in Librarian: Developing Library Outreach to University Residence Halls. *Reference & User Services Quarterly* 50, no. 1 (2010): 48–58.

1. Test Kitchen: Assessing Your Efforts

As the professionals at America's Test Kitchen know, any recipe can benefit from well-designed testing and thoughtful experimentation. Librarians bring the same high expectations to embedded instruction. Assessment is a cornerstone of any library curriculum. The recipes included here will guide you in creating an assessment plan for your embedded library instruction and will aid in demonstrating the value of embedded librarians.

Assessment Layer Cake:
Online Learning and Virtual Dessert

Helene Gold, Chair, Information Literacy and Research Department, Tallahassee Community College Library, goldh@tcc.fl.edu

NUTRITION INFORMATION

The goal of this recipe is to create a multi-layered assessment plan for our distance learning program. Although virtual dessert isn't as exciting as real-life dessert, it's still nice to have a reward at the end of a project.

COOKING TIME

Minimum one semester, but multiple semesters are recommended for long-term assessment data and comparisons.

INGREDIENTS AND EQUIPMENT

- Pre-test and post-test
- Research paper scoring rubric
- Student survey
- Faculty survey
- Screen capture or video creation software to create instructional videos
- Access to the learning management system (LMS)
- Familiarity with online learning environments

PREPARATION

- Identify faculty members who are willing to work with an embedded librarian and identify faculty members who will serve as the control group.
- Create pre and post tests.
- Create research paper sources rubric.
- Create or identify instructional videos that can be linked in the LMS.

COOKING METHOD

The embedded librarian will create a class page in the learning management system with handouts, YouTube videos, and other library instructional material. A pre-test of ten information literacy questions will be required during the first few days of the course and a post-test will be required during the last few days of the course. If there are in-person meetings, the librarian will meet with the class in the first couple of weeks to provide an introductory research overview (and cookies!). Students will be required to sign up individually or in groups to meet with the librarian in person either in the librarian's office, reference desk, or library lab for in-depth, focused research assistance (where once again, there will be cookies). Ideally, the initial meetings will have groups of fewer than five students in order for the librarian to work closely with students on individual research assignments. Each student should have his/her own computer/tablet.

A rubric will be used to assess student research papers, comparing the quality and use of sources. Papers from the embedded class will be compared to papers from online classes without an embedded librarian (similar to the assessment of the traditional English Composition 101 course) (See figure 1).

Student grades (collected as an anonymous list from the instructor) can be compared to other sections of the course without an embedded librarian to gauge the impact of the embedded librarian in the course.

ALLERGY WARNINGS

Because the pre and post tests are not graded, it is important for the instructor to require students to complete the assessment, perhaps in tandem with other required assignments.

CHEF'S NOTE

There may be instances when the online learners are unable to meet with the librarian in person. In this case, a synchronous learning session using the LMS chat/whiteboard or other online interactive group environments can be used for research consultation and guidance. If your library uses chat or text service, be sure the students have

FIGURE 1. Information Literacy Rubric: Bibliography/Source Evaluation (Undergraduate)

Unacceptable	Developing	Acceptable	Superior
• Student did not use any or used one or two sources • No exploration of periodical literature or books • All information sources are inappropriate, of poor quality and/or lack relevance • Sources have not undergone any peer or editorial review to ensure quality • Used no retrieval systems (online catalog or database) to locate sources • Demonstrates a lack of research sophistication overall	• Student used a limited number or limited variety of relevant source • Limited exploration of periodical literature or books Some information sources are inappropriate, of poor quality and/or lack relevance • Sources may have undergone peer or editorial review to ensure quality • Used one retrieval system to locate sources • Demonstrates low level of research sophistication overall	• Student used a variety of relevant sources but sources are not comprehensive • Exploration of outside periodical literature or books, but may have missed some useful sources • Information sources are appropriate, of good quality, and demonstrate relevance • Most sources have undergone peer or editorial review to ensure quality • Used multiple retrieval systems to locate sources • Demonstrates an acceptable level of research sophistication overall	• Student used a comprehensive variety of relevant sources • Exploration of periodical literature or books beyond what the assignment required • Information sources are highly appropriate, of excellent quality and demonstrate strong relevance • All sources have undergone peer or editorial review to ensure quality • Used multiple retrieval systems to locate sources. May have also used digital repositories, archival material, or other graduate-level retrieval systems. • Demonstrates high level of research sophistication overall

access to ALL librarian contact points. Some learners prefer telephone conversations while others prefer chat—and there will always be students who want to come to the library (be sure to have cookies for them!).

ADDITIONAL RESOURCES

- Chisholm, Elizabeth, and Heather M. Lamond. "Information Literacy Development At A Distance: Embedded Or Reality?" *Journal Of Library & Information Services In Distance Learning* 6.3/4 (2012): 224–234. Library, Information Science & Technology Abstracts with Full Text. Web. 24 July 2013.
- Edwards, Mary E., and Erik W. Black. "Contemporary Instructor-Librarian Collaboration: A Case Study Of An Online Embedded Librarian Implemen-

tation." *Journal Of Library & Information Services In Distance Learning* 6.3/4 (2012): 284–311. Library, Information Science & Technology Abstracts with Full Text. Web. 24 July 2013.

- Edwards, Mary, Swapna Kumar, and Marilyn Ochoa. "Assessing The Value Of Embedded Librarians In An Online Graduate Educational Technology Course." *Public Services Quarterly* 6.2/3 (2010): 271–291. Library, Information Science & Technology Abstracts with Full Text. Web. 1 May 2013.
- Hamilton, Buffy. *Embedded Librarianship: Tools and Practices*. Chicago : ALA TechSource, 2012. Print.
- Kumar, Swapna, and Mary E. Edwards. "Information Literacy Skills And Embedded Librarianship In An Online

Graduate Programme." *Journal Of Information Literacy* 7.1 (2013): 3–17. Library, Information Science & Technology Abstracts with Full Text. Web. 24 July 2013.

- Kvenild, Cassandra, and Kaijsa Calkins. *Embedded librarians: Moving Beyond One-shot Instruction*. Chicago: Association of College and Research Libraries, 2011. Print.
- Lyons, Tierney, and Michael M. Evans. "Blended Learning To Increase Student Satisfaction: An Exploratory Study." *Internet Reference Services Quarterly* 18.1 (2013): 43–53. Library, Information Science & Technology Abstracts with Full Text. Web. 24 July 2013.
- Matos, Michael A., Nobue Matsuoka-Motley, and William Mayer. "The

Embedded Librarian Online Or Face-To-Face: American University's Experiences." *Public Services Quarterly* 6.2/3 (2010): 130–139. Library, Information Science & Technology Abstracts with Full Text. Web. 1 May 2013

- Shell, Leslee, Steven Crawford, and Patricia Harris. "Aided And Embedded: The Team Approach To Instructional Design." *Journal Of Library & Information Services In Distance Learning* 7.1/2 (2013): 143–155. Library, Information Science & Technology Abstracts with Full Text. Web. 24 July 2013

- Tumbleson, Beth E. and John Burke. *Embedding Librarianship in Learning Management Systems: A How-to-do-it Manual for Librarians*. Chicago : Neal-Schuman, an imprint of the American Library Association, 2013. Print.

Marinated in Information Literacy:
Using Curriculum Mapping to Assess the Depth, Breadth, and Content of your Embedded Instruction Program

Leslie Bussert, Head of Teaching and Learning, University of Washington Bothell/Cascadia Community College, lbussert@uwb.edu

NUTRITION INFORMATION

The setting for this project is an undergraduate curriculum in which classroom and other modes of library instruction are regularly embedded across the degree programs. Goals:

- Engage in program-level assessment by mapping the integration of information literacy instruction across a curriculum, taking stock of the depth and breadth to which library instruction is incorporated into the classroom;
- Gain a stronger sense of the information literacy concepts and research tools taught across the curriculum;
- Identify areas where other modes of instruction may suffice or be a better fit (e.g. online instruction); and
- Examine opportunities for sharing or redistributing individual librarians' teaching responsibilities within the school.

SERVES

Librarians teaching in the school's degree programs and the instruction program administrator. Additional audiences may include the students, the library director, and the appropriate leadership within the school, such as deans, associate deans or department chairs.

COOKING TIME

This work can be done on a short or long timeframe, depending on the project goals, complexity of the curriculum being mapped, number of librarians involved, and the depth to which the mapping is conducted. Expect approximately 4 hours of information gathering and meeting preparation, 3.5 hours of working meetings and discussion, 2–4 hours for initial synthesis and analysis of data, and 3 hours of follow-up discussions with individual librarians and administrators.

INFORMATION DIETARY STANDARDS ADDRESSED

This recipe supports the following standards outlined in ACRL's Guidelines for Instruction Programs in Academic Libraries (http://www.ala.org/acrl/standards/guidelinesinstruction):

- I.B: Identification of content of instruction
- I.C: Identification of modes of instruction
- I.E: Evaluation and assessment

INGREDIENTS AND EQUIPMENT

- Google Docs Spreadsheet or a similar alternative
- Computer lab classroom or meeting room with laptops

PREPARATION (BEFORE THE PROJECT STARTS)

Generate goals or desired outcomes of the curriculum mapping in order to guide the process. For example, consider the following questions:

- What details about your information literacy curriculum do you hope to uncover and how can you obtain them?
- How will that information be useful?
- What discussions among librarians (and perhaps faculty) would you like this process or its results to generate?

Based on the project goals outlined, determine the information to be gathered in the curriculum maps. For example:

- Basic course information: title, size, frequency, degree(s) it serves, course type (e.g. required or elective)
- Instruction information:
  » Number of in-person classroom library instruction sessions offered
  » Course outcomes and/or assignments supported by the classroom library instruction
  » Desired information literacy out-

comes of the classroom library instruction

- » Library resources or tools taught (e.g. catalog, specific databases, etc.)
- » Activities through which the information literacy outcomes are met and resources are taught (e.g. concept mapping, self-paced worksheet, etc.)
- Program-level considerations:
  - » Is the course a good target for classroom library instruction? Why or why not?
  - » Are there alternative means for offering information literacy instruction in the course (e.g. collaboratively designed assignments with the faculty member, online tutorials, etc.)?

Gather useful curricular information and documents, such as:

- Lists and/or charts of courses in each degree program including course descriptions and designations (e.g. "core," "required" or "elective")
- Time schedules of courses to note class size and frequency
- Library instruction statistics from previous years
- Materials from the library instruction sessions (e.g. lesson plans, activity prompts, worksheets, etc.)
- Course assignments supported by the library instruction

COOKING METHOD

1. Prepare one shared Google Docs Spreadsheet with identical workbook tabs for each degree program being mapped. Having a shared document allows everyone to easily see each other's work and keeps the information in one file.
   a. For each workbook tab, list the predetermined informational prompts across the top as column headings (see Preparation section).
   b. Divide each workbook horizontally into three tiers or sections into which the courses being mapped can be classified:
      i. Tier 1: courses where in-person classroom library instruction is currently being offered
      ii. Tier 2: courses where library instruction or integration is accomplished through other means (such as co-designing assignments with faculty, student consultations, online research or class guides, and online tutorials)
      iii. Tier 3: courses that would be good candidates for library instruction but for which none is currently offered (for whatever reason)
2. Schedule a working meeting in a computer lab with the team of liaison librarians involved in the curricula being mapped. Explain the purpose of the exercise and allow librarians to begin populating the spreadsheet. Whatever is

not completed during this meeting can be finished individually by a designated deadline.

3. Optional: If possible, synthesize and analyze the data from each spreadsheet workbook in a visual manner. This offers a visual summary of the information literacy instruction across the entire curriculum that is easy to digest and understand. If you are fortunate enough to have access to a chart of the school/department's curriculum, use that as a starting point.
   a. Overlay the library instruction curriculum information onto the school/department's curriculum chart by first identifying all the courses for which some form of library instruction is offered, whether it be in the classroom or otherwise.
   b. Then, using the information entered into the librarian's spreadsheet workbooks, color code and highlight those courses based on the three tiers used to classify them during the mapping process (see Step 1b).
4. Plan a second meeting in a computer lab to facilitate discussion and understanding of the curriculum maps among the librarians. Materials required for this meeting are the curriculum maps, any visual summary of the maps generated, and a worksheet with prompts to guide librarians' review of the maps and discussion based on the project goals.

FIGURE 1. Information Literacy across the IAS Undergraduate Curriculum as of Fall 2011

First 90 credits Admission to all IAS undergrad degrees requires:			intermediate algebra (High School or college, no credit) 2 years of the same foreign language in high school or 10 credits through 102 of the same language in college 5 credits English composition; 5 credits quantitative and symbolic reasoning 15 credits in Visual, Literary & Performing Arts (VLPA), 15 in Individuals & Societies (I&S), 15 in Natural World (NW)*										
Degree-specific prerequisite credits			15					10		15		45	
Second 90 credits	AMS (BA)	CP (BA)	CLA (BA)	ES (BA)	GST (BA)	HR (minor)	IA (BA)	LEPP (option)	MCS (option)	STS (BA)	SEB (BA)	Env. Sci. (BS)	Other
# of students in degree (head count)**	12	155	65	52	120	82	10	19	154	18	165	21	
Program core	BIS 300: Introduction to Interdisciplinary Inquiry (5 credits)												
Degree core	One of BISAMS 363, 364 365, 366, 367, 368, 369	BISCP 343	One of BISCLA 318, 349, 360, 372, 380, 384	BIS 243, BES 301 or BIS 312, BES 312 or BIS 390, 5 cr econ, 5 cr env ethics	One of BISGST 303	BIS 353, BIS 403	BISIA 319	BISLEP301 BISLEP302	BISMCS 333	BISSTS 307	One of BISSEB 304, 331, 333, 359	BES: 301, 303, 312, BIS 315, 342 (27 credits) Plus 10-credit REN capstone or inde-pendent research	
Additional courses required for degree	BIS 312 or 340	BIS 312 and 315		10 credits pathway core			15 credits arts work-shops	BIS 315 and 5 more skills credits	35 credits, in 3 categor-ies Tier 1: BIS 313	BES 301 and BIS 315	One of BIS 312, 315, 410		
Degree elective credits	30 BIS 490	25	35 BIS 351, BIS 373, BIS 376	20 in 4 categories	35 BIS: 261-263,334, 340, 373, 376, 402, 403, BISAMS 363, BISGST 362 & 497	-- BISAMS 363	20 BIS 376, 373	20 in 2 categories BIS293	25 BES 485, BIS 240	30 BIS 340	40, structured by pathway BES 485		
Additional IAS credits		20		0					20			0	
General elective credits		22		27					22			10	BISSKL 375 BIS 232 (serves MTV deg. option?)
Program capstone	BIS 499: portfolio capstone (3 credits); students matriculated before Fall 2010 can take BIS 490 instead (5 credits)												

*In order to graduate, IAS students must complete a total of 25 credits in each Area of Knowledge (VLPA, I&S and NW). 10 of the 25 credits in each area must be completed through coursework taken at UW Bothell. The 10 Areas of Knowledge credits which must be taken at UW Bothell can be completed within the student's major requirements. Up to 35 credits of lower division (100–200 level) coursework taken at UW Bothell may be applied toward designated requirements within the 90 program credits.

Legend:
- = Offering classroom instruction
- = Would like to offer classroom instruction
- = Would like to pull back from classroom instruction
- = Offering consultations and/or online or other embedded instruction

"Research Methods" classes:
BES 301: Science Methods and Practice
BIS 312: Approaches to Social Research
BIS 340: Approaches to Cultural Research
BIS 410: Qualitative Inquiry

** Head count should be similar to FTE in terms of majors, but in terms of how many people take courses in each area, it is not that close a match (except in IA and Env Sci where prereqs narrow the numbers in the upper division work). – M. Groom 3/15/12

a. Have librarians review their peers' maps, spending about five minutes on each, while taking notes on the worksheet. After completing the review process, pair librarians up to discuss their findings and observations with each other and to continue adding to their notes.

b. Next, have librarians reflect individually on their own teaching and the information literacy curriculum in the degrees they support using the same worksheet to record notes. Below are some possible reflective prompts:

   » How has reviewing and discussing your peers' curriculum maps informed your approach to teaching in your degree area? Moving forward what might you change? What might the group consider changing?

   » Can you identify specific areas for action within your degree(s) this year? What are they and how might you accomplish them? What resources or support might you need to do so?

   » Lastly, this reflection should be followed up by a large group discussion to share findings, observations, suggestions for change, and next steps.

   » Collect and digitally scan the librarians' worksheets and return a copy to librarians for their own use. Follow up with individuals as needed to help them strategize how best to make changes or to identify the necessary resources for doing so.

5. Report out to your stakeholders, which may include your library director, deans and other administrators in the school/department, and faculty.

ALLERGY WARNINGS

- Clearly communicate the goals of the mapping project so librarians understand the value of engaging in the process and how the desired outcomes can positively impact the instruction program and their own teaching.

- Clearly communicate that this process is not meant to interrogate individual librarians' teaching loads or pedagogical choices. Instead, it is intended to assist with the group's collective understanding of how individual instruction activities fit together in an effort to thoughtfully and intentionally alter and scale the instruction program and teaching practice across the group.

- Do not have one individual do the analysis of the mapping data for the group! The value of this process lies with the whole group of librarians engaging in the synthesis and analysis in order to generate rich discussion and the sharing of ideas.

- When many users are simultaneously entering data into Google Spreadsheets it may freeze up momentarily from time to time. Alternative spreadsheet software could easily be substituted, though librarians may not be able to see each other's work in real time during the working meeting depending on its functionality.

CHEF'S NOTE

- Individually and collectively, this process can spur immediate changes to instruction and approaches to curriculum integration. Specific ideas for ways in which the group may alter classroom instruction surfaced and were agreed upon, individuals shared their ideas for making changes within their degree(s), and next steps were discussed, such as the possibility of folding our library's newly developed information literacy learning outcomes or continuing the discussion in meetings throughout the year.

- This exercise is very useful for orienting new librarians to the school's curriculum and our instructional role within it. Those new to the curriculum can use the maps to get a sense of their degrees, the courses they need to target, and what outcomes to strive for within them.

- The discussion among librarians may facilitate better understanding of what information literacy competencies and instruction look like in subject areas outside of their own or across interdisciplinary areas of study.

- Sharing the results, reflections, and issues surfaced by the process with faculty can generate rich discussion of the role of information literacy across the curriculum, and may assist opportunities for enacting necessary changes identified during the exercise.

- Follow-up work could include further conversations about information literacy outcomes taught too frequently across the curriculum or not at all. ACRL Information Literacy Standards or learning outcomes from the library and degree programs could facilitate this work.

ADDITIONAL RESOURCES
- Google Docs Spreadsheet: http://docs. google.com

A Three Course Meal (plus Dessert!):
Embedding Information Literacy into the First Year Seminar Curriculum

Lisa Coats, First Year Engagement Librarian, William Madison Randall Library, University of North Carolina Wilmington, coatsl@uncw.edu; Anne Pemberton, Associate Director, Library Assessment and Instructional Services, William Madison Randall Library, University of North Carolina Wilmington, pembertona@uncw.edu

NUTRITION INFORMATION

The primary goal of using the "three-course meal plus dessert" method is to connect with and provide instruction to first year students throughout their first semester utilizing a variety of means. Rather than only providing information literacy instruction during one instance, such as the typical one-shot session, librarians are able to provide instruction multiple times through the student's First Year Seminar (FYS) curriculum.

At the University of North Carolina Wilmington (UNCW), a three-course meal of information literacy instruction activities has been planned, cooked up, and dished into the required FYS curriculum. FYS has been designed as an information literacy-intensive course in UNCW's general education curriculum, due in part to the embedded information literacy activities cooked up and served by Randall Library Librarians. This feast engages students throughout the semester, which has ultimately provided students and librarians with an experience that is completely satisfying. There is also an optional dessert course for those FYS instructors and students who want even more!

COOKING TIME

- Prep work before gathering ingredients can vary
- One 50–75 minute face-to-face session for each section of FYS
- Assessment activities are ongoing and encourage constant improvement to the recipe

INFORMATION DIETARY STANDARDS ADDRESSED

- First Year Seminar Student Learning Objectives (FYS SLO)
- FYS SLO 2. Distinguish between popular and scholarly information resources.
- FYS SLO 1. List the differences between websites/broadcasts, newspapers, magazines, journals, and books.]
- FYS SLO 3. Select the appropriate tool to find a book and an article on a particular topic.
- FYS SLO 4. Identify appropriate service points for assistance both in the library and via the library's website.
- FYS SLO 5. Apply established evaluation criteria to determine if an information source is appropriate.

INGREDIENTS AND EQUIPMENT

- A collaborative relationship with the department that is responsible for FYS is a primary ingredient for this recipe. Librarians who want to try this recipe would first want to establish this relationship.
- Librarians who have been trained to teach the face-to-face session.
- In addition to the textbook chapter, the following is needed:
  - » Online quiz or online form creation (through SurveyMonkey or other tool)
  - » Computer access for all students
  - » Instructor workstation
  - » Presentation software (such as PowerPoint or Prezi)

PREPARATION

- Students should have purchased the FYS textbook as it is required for the course.
- Librarians should have at least a pinch of enthusiasm, and more than a dash of interest in student engagement, before teaching the face-to-face session!

COOKING METHOD

First Course: Textbook and Quiz

- Students are required by their FYS instructor to read their FYS textbook chapter about the library (authored by librarians). The chapter includes an overview of the library's services and collections; how to create effective keyword searches; and differences between types of publications. Screen shots of the library's website show specific tools that can be used for searching for articles and books. Evaluating information and citing information are also discussed in the chapter.

- Students complete an online quiz assessing their retention of the chapter. The quiz is housed on the library's web server and allows librarians to quickly determine which concepts seem to be problematic for students.

Second Course: Face-to-face Library Instruction

- Students complete an anonymous, online questionnaire that serves the dual purpose of challenging their preconceptions about their research skills, as well as providing useful information to librarians about students' knowledge of concepts and previous research experience.

- Librarians serve up interactive instruction on the various types of publications available to them; the difference between "popular" and "scholarly"

FIGURE 1. Library Website Exercise

Library Website Exercise

Librarians are doing research on how people use the Library's website. We appreciate your participation! Your voluntary answers on this worksheet are part of the research and should be anonymous, so please do not put your name on this worksheet. Thanks!

Using Library Search Tools (http://library.uncw.edu/)

ARTICLES

1. Search for an article on the <u>BP gulf oil spill</u> in the search box under "Articles & eResources." List the <u>specific types</u> of publications that you find in your search:

2. How is this search tool different from Google (in terms of the *types* of results you retrieve)?

[STOP HERE UNTIL FURTHER NOTICE]

BOOKS AND MORE

1. Using the "Books & More" search tab, find **Eli Saslow's** book *Ten Letters*.

    a. What formats of this book does the Library have? _____

    b. List the call number for a print copy: _____

2. What is the title of a DVD about "cyberbullying" _____

    a. How long is this DVD? _____

    b. What floor in the library is this DVD located on? (*Hint: Click on DVD "Location"*) _____

[STOP HERE UNTIL FURTHER NOTICE]

Finding Information on the Library Website (http://library.uncw.edu/)

1. What time does the library close on Wednesday, November 21, 2012? _____

2. What are the Learning Commons Help Desk (Reference) hours for September 14, 2012? _____

3. How many books can you check out from the General Collection? _____
(*Hint: Look under "Information for: Freshmen/First Year"*)

4. On what floor of the Library is the General Collection? _____
List the steps you took to find this on the Library's website:

Randall Library, University of North Carolina Wilmington

FIGURE 2. CRITIC Exercise

		CRITIC EXERCISE: After examining the source thoroughly, answer the following questions in the space provided.
CLAIM	1	Summarize the claim, or main point, of the author(s) in two to three sentences.
RELIABILITY OF AUTHOR	2	a. Is an author or are authors listed? *Circle: Yes / No* (If you answered "No," describe how this impacts the reliability of the source in two to three sentences.) b. If an author is listed, is the author reliable? *Circle: Yes / No* (Justify your answer by listing at least three reasons why the author is reliable or unreliable.)
INFORMATION BACKING THE CLAIM	3	Describe, in two to three sentences, what information the author uses to back his or her claim. [Questions to consider: Did the author review previous research? Did the author conduct interviews? Did the author conduct a study? Does the author cite statistical information? Does the source have a list of references?]
TESTING	4	List three ways you could test the author's claim. [Questions to consider: What type of research could you do on your own? What additional sources might you consult? How could you replicate the author's research methods?]
INTENDED AUDIENCE	5	a. Describe the specific audience the author(s) likely had in mind when the source was written. [Questions to consider: Was the source written for the general public? Was it written for professionals or researchers in a particular field? If so, which field?] b. What type of source is this? *Circle: Scholarly / Popular* (Justify your answer by listing at least three reasons why the source is scholarly or popular.)
CONCLUSION	6	a. Keeping your previous answers in mind, summarize your conclusion about the quality of this source in one or two sentences. b. Identify and discuss which elements of the CRITIC model were most important to you in drawing your final conclusion in two to three sentences.

The CRITIC assignment was adapted from:
Helmke, J. & Matthies B. (2004). Using the CRITIC Acronym to Teach Information Evaluation. *LOEX Conference.*

sources; how to utilize library search tools to identify and locate these publications; and how to evaluate information.

- In pairs, students complete two worksheets. The first worksheet (figure 1) requires that students use the introductory information they gained from the textbook chapter to search for books, articles, and information about Randall Library using the library's website. The second worksheet (figure 2) requires students to evaluate a source using the "CRITIC" model and evaluate a source using the model and the questions provided on the worksheet.

Third Course: Evaluating Information Assignment

- Outside of class, students complete a required assignment to evaluate a scholarly article, a popular article, and a website using the CRITIC model that was discussed in the textbook chapter and during the face-to-face session.
- The assignment is delivered online.
- Once an assignment is submitted, a message is automatically generated for the student's FYS instructor. As with the quiz, the assignment is hosted on the library's web server and librarians use this assignment for assessment.

Dessert: Optional tour

Some students and FYS instructors may feel quite full after the three-course meal. But for those that are still a little hungry, librarians offer dessert! FYS instructors can (and do!) have their students get even more acquainted with the library by having students complete the Randall Library online virtual tour, or by having their FYS "Link" (a sophomore student mentor who works with each section of FYS) provide a tour of the library using the tour script written by Randall Library librarians. Both methods ensure that accurate information is delivered to FYS students.

ALLERGY WARNINGS

- Like any good recipe you create from scratch, it takes trial and error to determine the right mix of ingredients. Be prepared to continually taste your dishes and know that you'll likely need to adjust this or that.
- Being willing to have the soufflé or cake flop a few times while you try!

CHEF'S NOTE

The three-course meal (plus dessert!) has proven to be an excellent way to establish a connection to FYS students. The activities are truly embedded within the FYS curriculum rather than simply being an "add-on" or a "guest lecture." Having a textbook chapter indicates the importance of the library for FYS students and a quiz on the chapter reinforces the importance of the content. Questionnaires, discussion prompts, worksheets and other hands-on activities are some of the ingredients that have proven to be a successful second course in both engaging and empowering first semester undergraduate students in the learning process during a required face-to-face session. In all sessions, assessment is a critical component, so both students and instructors have helped refine this recipe. The out-of-class assignment in the third course provides students a chance to implement what they have ingested in the other courses. Finally, through a survey and informal discussions, librarians have been able to review the recipe helping to inspire long-term revision of the instructional curriculum.

ADDITIONAL RESOURCES

- First Year Library Survival Guide: http://library.uncw.edu/guides/freshman_seminar

2. Menu Planning: Creating a Long Term Plan for Embedded Instruction

Putting the pieces together once you have developed a successful embedded instruction initiative takes careful planning and evaluation. Do you require a scalable effort to embed in every online course? Or perhaps you want to automate some of your work to reduce staff hours in instruction? We have gathered successful long range ideas from librarians who know the ropes.

Conversion Recipe:
From Tableside Service to Buffet Style—Shifting a Micro Embedded Model to Macro

Jennie Simning, Librarian, Hennepin Technical College, jennie.simning@hennepintech.edu; Erika Bennett, Supervisor of Instruction Services Team, Capella University Library, erika.bennett@capella.edu

NUTRITION INFORMATION

Embedding a librarian directly into the online courseroom to provide individualized research assistance and information literacy instruction is a very time-consuming and ultimately un-scalable embedded model for many libraries.[1,2] This recipe allows you to retain the value of embedding information literacy instruction in the courseroom, save staff time, and reach larger populations of students by creating a macro-level embedded model: a guided, assessment-driven information literacy website that can be embedded within any online courseroom.

Micro Embedded Model: Embedding into the online courseroom in such a way that research assistance and librarian interactions are very individualized—typically reaching or responding to one student at a time.

Macro Embedded Model: Embedding into the online courseroom in such a way that research assistance can be provided to many students at once, typically using a guide, website or other resource rather than a direct librarian interaction.

SERVES

This serves an infinite number of students. The conversion moves the model from a staff-limited capacity to a media-based, fully scalable option.

COOKING TIME

Three months from scratch. Shorter if ingredients are prepped in advance.

INGREDIENTS AND EQUIPMENT

- Student FAQs from micro-level embedded model
- Aged PRIMO®-recognized research skills website[3,4] (or generic non-brand content of choice)
- Scalability report, justifying the shift to stakeholders
- Faculty buy-in (for presentation of dish)
- 2 librarians with embedded and media design experience
- Interactive/media designers
- Web production team
- Project manager (optional)
- Curriculum specialist (optional)
- Instructional designer (optional)
- Web content editor (optional)
- User experience analyst (optional)

PREPARATION

If available, solicit the resources that your school would normally dedicate to creating a new online course. At our institution, a course slot allotment was applied for, which granted us 100s of dedicated pre-funded hours with a curriculum specialist, instructional designer, project manager, web production team, assessment specialist, web content editor and user experience analyst.

Once the resources have been acquired, the librarians should define the learning outcomes for instructional website with assistance of curriculum specialist, then host an initial kick-off meeting with all involved parties to discuss their roles and expectations for the project. At the kick-off meeting, the intended audience and scope of the content should be defined, and a decision on who will design which media elements and who will spearhead content writing should be made.

COOKING METHOD

The main cooking techniques include instructional design team & budget, navigational assessments, pre- and post- instruction assessments, learning media & interactive tutorials.

FIGURE 1. Library Research & Information Literacy Skills site. This main page includes links to the four major skill areas as well as to pre- and post-assessments.

Library Research & Information Literacy Skills

Information literacy requires you to *recognize when information is needed and have the ability to locate, evaluate, and ethically communicate information* (ALA, 1989). These are vital skills in our rapidly-changing, information-driven world, at the core of your scholarly journey, and are expected to be mastered by the time you graduate.

Two recommended options for using this section:

1. Begin with the first section and progress through to the end.
2. Complete the self- assessment to determine your areas of strength and areas for improvement. Then review the appropriate sections, as needed.

You should have enough understanding of each subject area to score highly on the final assessment.

Identifying scholarly resources

Learn to find scholarly resources, what "peer-review" means, how to identify peer-reviewed sources, and the difference between primary and secondary sources.

Defining your topic

Learn strategies for selecting and focusing a research topic. Tips for refining a topic that is too broad or too narrow are provided.

Searching effectively

Find out how to plan and construct a research strategy; how to choose a database, select the best keywords, and build an effective search; and how to refine your search.

Evaluating source quality

Learn how to evaluate sources in the library and on the Internet, and see how your information literacy skills can benefit you in the workplace.

Citation: ALA Presidential Committee on Information Literacy. (1989, January 10). Presidential committee on information literacy: Final report. Retrieved from http://www.ala.org/ala/mgrps/divs/acrl/publications/whitepapers/presidential.cfm

Resources

Tour of the Library

❯ **Tour the Library**

Information Skills Assessments

Initial Self-Assessment

This self-assessment will help you see what your Information Literacy skills level is, and will recommend areas within this site to help you improve.

❯ **Take the self- assessment**

Final Assessment

Once you have reviewed and feel comfortable with the research skills on this site, take the final assessment and test what you've learned.

❯ **Take the final assessment**

Embedded Model Creation

1. Website Structure
   - The librarian creates learning outcomes (based on ACRL Information Literacy standards) for the instructional website. This can be done with the support of the curriculum specialist (optional).
   - The librarian then works with web production team, the instructional designer (optional) and the project manager (optional) to turn the learning outcomes into a wireframe* for the website *(See Vocabulary Notes).
   - Tip: If sanctioned by a usability expert (optional), try dividing each learning outcome into its own section of the website. This allows students to choose from specific skills they may want to review and aids in the creation of a navigational assessment for the site content (see Step 4).

2. Website Text Creation
   - The librarian working on contact creation can then take any FAQs or template answers that may have been saved from a micro-level embedded model and combine them with old material from aging information literacy tutorials or instruction materials to generate new content.
   - If the web production team has created copy decks* (based on wireframe) for the librarian *(See Vocabulary Notes), the librarian can populate the copy decks with the newly created text content.
   - The librarian should then send content to others on the instructional design team for review and approval.

3. Website Media Creation
   - The librarian works with dedicated interactive/media designers to script and storyboard any new media being created for the site.
   - The interactive/media designers (or librarian if no dedicated designers are available) then create media using Captivate or other media creation program.

4. Assessment Creation/Data Gathering
    - The librarian begins the assessment creation process by writing the content of the initial, navigational assessment for the instructional site. In this experience-based assessment, students typically answer a series of questions about their current understanding and use of various information literacy skills covered in the tutorial.
    - The librarian then writes the content for the final assessment which students will complete after reviewing the site to test what they have learned.
    - Once the content is complete, the librarian works with interactive/media designers and the web production team to turn the assessment content into an online quiz. For a more individualized experience, see if the design or production team can use branch scripting, so that the assessment results will recommend starting points or areas of focus/review within the website, based on a student's responses.
    - Data gathering tips: Consider implementing the following:
        » Ask the assessment design team to set-up the assessments so that the librarian is emailed the results each time an assessment is taken. For the librarian, it helps to set-up dedicated folders in your email where these results can be routed.
        » If available, the librarian can then export the assessment data within the emailed results to an Excel .csv file.
        » Macros in Microsoft Excel can be used to parcel out data into a usable format.
        » Consider adding identifying information to the instructional assessments (i.e. degree, program of study, new student, etc.) to aid data analysis
        » Please see "Allergy Warning" on data gathering.

5. Finalizing Website
    - The librarian reviews all media and assessments with interactive designers to ensure assessments are created correctly and data is being harvested appropriately.
    - The librarian or web production team should send all content within the copy deck (text, media, assessments) to web content editor (optional) for a final review.
    - When content is approved, the librarian works with web production team to turn the copy deck into reality.
    - Once site is hosted online, the librarian should review all content again before going live.

6. Promotion and Outreach
    - Once the site is live, the librarian should create promotional materials to share with faculty and students.
    - The librarian should also partner with faculty to pilot the site and begin gathering data to support further faculty buy-in.
    - Tip: As this site is being piloted, the librarian will find it helpful to gather qualitative data from student and instructor feedback in the courseroom and quantitative data from the assessments.
    - Once promotional materials are created and site has been piloted, the librarian should create an outreach plan to communicate the success and availability of the new instructional website to other faculty and departments. See "Presentation and Garnishing" for ideas on courseroom inclusion.

7. Website Revision
    - Using qualitative and quantitative data gathered from embedded courses and from assessment responses, the librarian may continue to revise the site content or assessments as necessary.

Presentation And Garnishing

To present your new embedded website in the online courseroom, work with the course faculty to create an information literacy-based assignment around the site. Two presentation options might include:

1. Students review the site and complete assessments. Then they utilize what they learned through hands-on practice (i.e. find articles in a database). Finally, they reflect on the website and their hands-on experience with other students in a course discussion post where they can

share tips, important takeaways, remaining questions, etc.

2. Create several small information literacy assignments throughout the course, embedding the corresponding section of the website at the point of need in the courseroom (i.e. assign section on "Defining a Topic" when they are picking topics, assign section on "Searching Effectively" when they need to find articles for a paper). With this presentation option, consider assigning "Final Assessment" of the website toward the beginning and at the end of the course to see how scores improve.

Garnishments for your dish may include:
- Additional student worksheets to accompany website content.
- Recommended practice activities after each section of the site.

If possible, we recommend that you integrate your instructional site into the curriculum of the course. This may be done by tying the learning outcomes you have established to the course competencies outlined for the course. This is particularly effective for courses early in a student's program when they are expected to begin building skills for defining, finding, and using information.

ALLERGY WARNINGS

Once the site is created, faculty partnership or faculty buy-in is essential for embedding your new website in the courseroom. To pilot your new site, try partnering with the faculty you worked with in your micro-level model.

You may also wish to consult a user experience analyst or conduct user experience testing prior to launching your website, as there may be recommended user revisions prior to going live. We did not complete this step in cooking our dish.

If you host the final dish inside your virtual campus, behind an authentication system, it won't be eligible for renewed PRIMO recognition.

With the automated data gathering from the assessments—beware! You may be inundated with more data than you have the time to analyze. It will help to parcel out the meaningful data from the non- meaningful.

CHEFS' NOTE

If this recipe is well-executed, the only danger is that it can be too popular. We keep receiving word that new courses have added the media pieces and assessments, but if/when the course development teams don't collaborate with us on the assignment design, they often don't give students adequate preparation and practice with the search activities. The ease and speed of adopting the embedded model can lead to some unanticipated, less effective iterations. See the supplement to David Shumaker's *Models of Embedded Librarianship Final Report* from SLA.org for the extended details on this conversion project. We are Site #5.[5]

VOCABULARY NOTES:

WIREFRAMES—brief outline, skeletal framework or schematics for a website.

COPY DECK—Normally, consists of a blueprint of the main structure and headings of a website. It should outline the navigation and graphics and general flow of the site in a format that can be populated with text content.

NOTES

1. Bennett, Erika, and Jennie Simning. "Embedded Librarians and Reference Traffic: A Quantitative Analysis." *Journal of Library Administration* 50 (2010): 443–457.

2. Myers, Glenda. "The Embedded Library: A Marriage Made in Heaven or in Hell?" *2013 IATUL Proceedings.* Accessed June 25, 2013. http://docs.lib.purdue.edu/iatul/2013/papers/34.

3. Association of College & Research Libraries (ACRL). "Peer-Reviewed Instructional Materials Online (PRIMO)." Accessed June 25, 2013. http://www.ala.org/acrl/aboutacrl/directoryofleadership/sections/is/iswebsite/projpubs/primo.

4. Capella University Library. "Library Research Handbook: Your Roadmap to Information Literacy." Accessed June 25, 2013. http://www.capella.edu/interactivemedia/informationLiteracy/index.aspx.

5. Shumaker, David. "Models of Embedded Librarianship: Addendum 2011." Grant paper, Special Library Association, 2011. Accessed June 25, 2013. http://embeddedlibrarian.files.wordpress.com/2013/04/modelsofembeddedlibrarianshipaddendum2011corrected.pdf.

Library Widget for the Learning Management System (with a Dash of Contextual Relevance)

Mike Flakus, Lead Web Programmer, Portland State University, mflakus@pdx.edu; Amy R. Hofer, Distance Learning Librarian, Portland State University, ahofer@pdx.edu

NUTRITION INFORMATION

The library widget is a collection of bookmarks that provide a portal to library content with a very small footprint on the course home page. This software enables you to automatically embed access to the most relevant course-specific library resources available.

SERVES

The entire online campus!

COOKING TIME

Depends on how many extra flavors you include in your widget. Vanilla widget can be prepared in under 60 minutes.

INGREDIENTS AND EQUIPMENT

- Portland State University Library's Open-Source Library Widget
- Learning Management System (LMS): we use Desire2Learn (D2L)
- Web Server with PHP installed—to host the widget and collect stats
- Buy-in from the people that make decisions about default course home pages in the LMS

SAUCE

A research guide system with tagging or API (our code is fully integrated with LibGuides) Memcache or MySQL—to improve loading performance

PREPARATION

- Download the application files and installation instructions for the Portland State University Library's Open-Source Library Widget
- Tag research guides with subject and/ or course codes. We created a spreadsheet that helped us map subject prefixes used in the course catalog to our existing research guides. (For more information on guide tags, see "Chef's Notes".)

COOKING METHOD

- Copy Portland State University Library's Open-Source Library Widget files to a web server.
- Edit config.inc.php to select which features to display and add links to other tools
  - » Adjust the catalog search box to link to your library's catalog
  - » Adjust the contact links to suit your needs for your library
  - » Optional LibGuides Integration: Set your LibGuides institutional ID

  - » Optional Caching: Set the location of your memcache server or create a MySQL database and set the location and authentication information for that database.
- Create a widget box in your LMS and load the widget via dynamic external CSS and JavaScript includes. You will want to include special tokens in the script source for the course code, course name and role of the viewing patron.

Example Widget for Desire2Learn LMS:

```
<link rel="stylesheet" type="text/
css" href="https://myinstitution.edu/
widget.css" /> <script src="https://
myinstitution.edu/widget.php?course_
code={OrgUnitCode}&course_
name={OrgUnitName}&r ole_
name={RoleCode}" type="text/javascript" />
```

- Adjust HTML/CSS design to taste!
- After the widget has been taste tested for a variety of courses, invite your LMS administrator to add your widget box to the default course template so the library's presence will exist on every course homepage.

FIGURE 1. Library widget, indicating when viewed on a course guide

we tag our course guides with the course prefix and course number and our subject guides with appropriate course prefixes. For instance, BA 301's course guide would be tagged with "BA 301" or "BA 301-001" and the Business subject guide might be tagged with "BA", "MGMT", "ACTG", "FIN", etc., to match against all relevant course prefixes. These tags can be entered in LibGuides under Guide Settings > Change Guide Information > Assigned Tags.

ALLERGY WARNINGS

When our widget was added to the default university course template, we accidentally ignited a flambé as tens of thousands of widget views occurred each day. This caused SpringShare to contact us to confirm that the dramatic increase in API usage was intentional. To lessen the load on the LibGuides API we've now integrated caching, which has brought the load of API requests back down to a simmer.

CHEFS' NOTES

The library is getting significant exposure from the widget's presence on the default course home page. At Portland State University, course homepages in D2L get more views than all the pages in the Library's website combined! All the same, our click-through rate could improve. Students are mainly clicking on the contextually aware link to the most relevant course or subject guide, which suggests that the widget would be even more useful with more course-specific content. Here are some of the ideas we hope will make our widget even tastier in the next version:

- Display direct links to course reserves items
- Add a live search box for popular article databases
- Allow faculty to customize their course's widget
  » Enable faculty to customize the look and feel of the widget for their course
  » Enable faculty to add links to recommended databases
  » Enable faculty to add links to recommended web resources with explanatory text

When mixing in LibGuides, or a comparable substitute, it will be important to tag your guides in such a way that you can identify the best match for each course. For the best final presentation, it's best to first check for an exactly matching course guide for the specific course code. If an exact match cannot be found, then you'll want to fall back to one or more relevant subject guides for the course discipline. In the case where there are no appropriate guides to display, we simply link to our subject guide index page. To achieve this cascading effect,

ADDITIONAL RESOURCES

- Portland State University Library's Open-Source Library Widget: https://code.google.com/p/pdx-contextually-aware-library-widget
- Hofer, A.R., & Flakus, M. (2012, February 10). *Library widget in the LMS: Way cooler than it sounds.* Lightning talk at Online Northwest, Corvallis OR. Presentation slides available from http://www.ous.edu/onlinenw/2012/presentations/hofer.pptx
- Hofer, A.R. (2012, February 23). *Taking the library to the LMS: A collaborative solution for online classrooms.* Poster session at 2012 EDUCAUSE West/Southwest Regional Conference, Portland OR. Online handout available from http://tinyurl.com/psuwidget
- Hofer, A.R., & Munro, K. (2013). Energy efficiency in the LMS: Faculty evaluations of a sustainable embedded model. E. Leonard and E. McCaffrey (Eds.), *Virtually embedded: Case studies of online embedded librarianship.* Chicago: ACRL Press.

Culinary School:
Fundamentals of Library Cuisine For Faculty

Ariana Baker, Distance Learning Librarian, Kimbel Library, Coastal Carolina University, abaker@coastal.edu

NUTRITION INFORMATION

Many librarians would like to embed in every course offered by their college or university, but there are a finite number of classes where we can actually do so. In addition, there are many classes where a thorough information literacy session or tutorial isn't necessary, but where students can benefit from access to library owned resources, in particular online journals and streaming videos. The goal of this project is to teach instructors enough information so that they can incorporate library resources into their classes themselves.

These tutorials can be subject-specific or relevant across the curriculum. While tutorials created for students are generally geared towards classes with a research component, these faculty tutorials can be beneficial for anyone who wants to incorporate the library's subscription resources into their course management system.

SERVES
Unlimited

COOKING TIME
Preparation: Expect each recipe to take about three hours to create, at least in the beginning. This includes writing the script, rehearsing to make sure the script accurately reflects what you want to teach, recording the screencast, and editing the screencast. Cooking Time: This should last no more than five minutes. The tutorials should be brief and to the point. Create additional tutorials to explain other important information, rather than covering a lot of material in one tutorial. For example, faculty may need a brief overview of searching the library website or searching different databases before they can retrieve library resources to use in their classes. Divide the tutorials by topics if they are in danger of exceeding five minutes. Remember, it's not only too many cooks, but also too many ingredients, that can spoil the broth.

INGREDIENTS AND EQUIPMENT
- Computer
- Screencasting software
- Microphone

PREPARATION
Create a brief script (no more than two single-spaced pages) that explains your lesson. For example, instructors at your college or university may need to know a) how to find permanent URLs to database articles and ebooks, b) how to use that URL to link to the article from within a course management system, and c) what your library's proxy prefix is and why it's necessary. Use the script to create a screencast that you can upload to a website for instructors to view. Repeat the process to create tutorials for finding and linking to and/or embedding subscription streaming videos in a course management system, and other topics that you think may be valuable to instructors in an online environment. (See figure 1.)

COOKING METHOD
Be thorough when creating these tutorials. If you're concerned that a video tutorial is too long, split it up into segments. For example, some databases may have a proxy prefix built into the link and others may not. You can create two separate tutorials to explain how to link to each type of database article. You may also want to explain how to link to streaming videos in one tutorial, and how to embed them in another. The recipe is adaptable and can make one large or many small tutorials.

Suggested topics (either for individual tutorials or inclusion in more comprehensive tutorials):
- Finding the correct links and embed

codes for linking to and embedding library resources (electronic books and journal articles and streaming videos)

- Understanding and finding proxy URLs in the article, book, or video link
- Adding the materials to your course management system

FIGURE 1. Kimbel Library's faculty tutorial webpage

The topics above assume that instructors know how to search your library's website. However, be aware that this is not always the case. For this reason, it may be helpful to provide a short overview of the search process before transitioning to the main topic of your tutorial.

Instruction session: It is not necessary to hold a face-to-face instruction session, since instructors can view the videos on their own time. However, instructors should be made aware of these tutorials via email notifications or mailed letters/newsletters. In addition, brief presentations at department meetings and other faculty meetings can be a great way to get the word out.

Access: Both students and faculty should be able to access all library screencasts on a designated tutorials webpage. Linking to the tutorials from various department websites and libguides can also help you reach your users at point of need.

Technical Tips

1. Depending on the software you use, you may have the option to add captioning. Be careful though, because captions sometimes cover the parts of the screen you want your viewers to see. An alternative is to create printable directions with screenshots, which will help faculty to follow along with the tutorials.

Faculty Tutorials

Finding and Linking to Subscription Database Articles in Your Course Management System (Part 1) (3:26)

This tutorial explains how to find articles in Kimbel Library's EBSCO databases, find permanent URLs for those articles, and link to the articles from your Blackboard or Moodle course.

Finding and Linking to Subscription Database Articles in Your Course Management System (Part 2) (3:35)

This tutorial explains how to find articles in Kimbel Library's non-EBSCO databases, find permanent URLs for those articles, add a proxy prefix to the articles for off-site access, and link to the articles from your Blackboard or Moodle course.

Linking and Embedding Subscription Videos in Your Course Management System (4:17)

This tutorial explains how to find streaming videos from *Films on Demand*, find the permanent URL and embed code for those videos, and link to or embed the videos within your Blackboard or Moodle course.

Top of Page

Questions?

If you have any questions or comments about these tutorials please contact Distance Learning Librarian Ariana Baker. Having trouble playing videos? Please make sure you have a recent update of Adobe Flash Player.

2. Keep your highlighting and zooming to a minimum. Both can be great tools to help demonstrate a feature on your website, but too much of either can distract from your lesson.

3. Keep your videos short, under five minutes each. If your faculty sees long tutorials, they may think using library resources will be arduous or time-consuming. Short tutorials can be a great opportunity to demonstrate how quick and easy it can be to use library resources.

Suggested Software

*   Jing: Jing is a free download that is best if you don't need to make major edits to your tutorial. Jing does have some editing capabilities but not as much as subscription screencasting software.
*   Screencast-o-matic: There are both free and subscription versions of this software. The annual subscription is relatively inexpensive and includes editing capabilities such as captioning, zooming and highlighting. Users can save to the screencast-o-matic website and then link to those videos in their course management system.
*   Camtasia: This subscription screencasting software provides full editing capabilities and allows users to save to the web (screencast.com) or download to your computer. Screencast.com has the added benefit of including embed codes so users can easily embed the videos directly into anther website or course management system.

ALLERGY WARNINGS

1. While tutorials should be as thorough as possible, there will inevitably be some topics that are not covered, as well as differences among various databases that are not all discussed. Be sure to provide contact information so that faculty can reach out to you if they need more help.

2. Websites change a lot, so be sure to occasionally review the process to verify that the instructions are still correct. Not only databases, but also course management systems, often make upgrades that could create confusion when the screencasts don't match what instructors actually see.

ADDITIONAL RESOURCES

For an example of a tutorial webpage, you may want to view Kimbel Library's tutorials at http://www.coastal.edu/library/tutorials.

A La Carte Library Instruction:
Empowering Faculty to Teach Information Literacy

Jason Vance, Middle Tennessee State University, Jason.Vance@mtsu.edu Amy York, Middle Tennessee State University, Amy.York@mtsu.edu

NUTRITION INFORMATION

To accommodate the growing number of instruction requests from faculty who teach Fundamentals of Communication (a.k.a. public speaking), the librarians created an *a la carte* menu of self-serve library instruction tools to enable classroom faculty to teach information literacy without a librarian.

This project was designed to assist faculty who teach freshman/sophomore general education public speaking classes. Roughly 75–80 sections are offered each semester. This approach may translate well to other high volume general education courses that have standardized learning outcomes.

SERVES
15–20 faculty members

COOKING TIME
This project is updated and reintroduced each semester. The initial training takes place as part of the department's faculty meeting, and typically lasts 20–30 minutes.

INGREDIENTS AND EQUIPMENT
- Secret website
- Downloadable and customizable PowerPoint lecture with screenshots (and a low-fi version)
- Student handout
- Student worksheet
- Instructional videos
- LibGuide

COOKING METHOD
Working with representatives from the academic department, the librarians came up with some mutually agreed-upon learning outcomes. In our case, the chief learning outcome was that students should be able to select and use appropriate tools in order to find quality information on current events in support of their researched speeches. The librarians created the new PowerPoint lectures, handout, and worksheet, and made them available for download. The LibGuide and instructional videos were repurposed from previous uses. All of these were compiled in one place to create an *a la carte,* self-service menu for faculty.

ALLERGY WARNING
Focusing the PowerPoint files and handouts on particular databases, as we did, means that they will need to be updated as interfaces or resource holdings change.

Because many instructors embed the slides in course management systems, getting them swapped out for newer versions may be challenging.

CHEFS' NOTE
We had a very low response rate to a survey that we sent to speech instructors about the course materials, however, the LibGuide for this course was viewed over 3,000 times in the most recent semester. During this semester only 17 of nearly 100 sections came to the library for instruction from a librarian, so this high usage indicates that instructors are sharing the resources with their students themselves. Because the LibGuide is viewed so often, we added a tab for instructor resources in addition to offering them at the separate website, which is viewed far less often.

ADDITIONAL RESOURCES
- PowerPoint files and handouts: http://library.mtsu.edu/reference/comm2200
- LibGuide: http://libraryguides.mtsu.edu/comm2200

Don't Bite Off More Than You Can Chew!
Creating a Sustainable Embedded Librarian Service for Academic Libraries

Jessica Mussell, Instruction and Public Services Librarian, Royal Roads University, Victoria, BC, Canada, jessica.mussell@royalroads.ca

NUTRITION INFORMATION

This recipe provides guidance and ideas to institutions with a small complement of librarians to manage an online embedded service in a sustainable manner. It is geared towards libraries that are looking to start an embedded librarian service or alter their current service to make it more sustainable in the long-run.

SERVES

Serves any online course that has a research component, regardless of class size.

COOKING TIME

Servicing an embedded librarian program is ongoing and is managed year-round based on need.

INGREDIENTS AND EQUIPMENT

- Access to an online learning management system (LMS)
- Librarians, with one librarian acting as the lead to manage the embedding requests
- Support from instructional designers/ course instructors (as needed)

PREPARATION

No library has enough librarians to cover every course at an institution, and realistically not every course will even need a librarian, so be very selective in the courses your library plans to target to keep it manageable workload-wise. Here are some tips to guide you:

1. **Be strategic with course selection**— Identify courses where students have an assignment which requires them to do research. Some examples might be:
   a. Literature review assignments for doctoral-level or graduate-level courses;
   b. Capstone or graduating projects for undergraduate-level courses; or
   c. Courses with a market-research/ legal-research component.
2. **Be strategic with resources**—Identify a lead librarian to manage the embedded librarian requests and promote the service to identified courses. Typically this role will fall to the instructional librarian; however it can be anyone who is up for the task. The lead librarian will be responsible for scheduling embedding requests among the librarian complement to ensure equal distribution of requests so that no one librarian is overloaded, and ideally so that a librarian is only embedded in one course at a time.

3. **Be strategic with time**—Keep the length of embedded time to something manageable like a maximum of one work week (4–5 days), and only embed librarians in a course at the point where their services are most needed. This means choosing days when students are most likely to be embarking on some form of research that will require them to utilize the library's resources and they are most likely to have research-related questions.

COOKING METHOD

A librarian assigned to a course should:
1. Review the research assignment and have a discussion with the course instructor in advance of being embedded to go over any expectations or concerns they might have, clarify assignment outcomes, and to ensure an "Ask-a-Librarian" discussion forum is set up in the course with appropriate access privileges. (See figure 1.)
2. Have some draft posts ready to publish to the "Ask-a-Librarian" discussion forum. This could include a "welcome" post inviting students to ask questions, a few posts around strategies for constructing searches (e.g. broadening/ narrowing searches), one around evalu-

FIGURE 1. Screenshot of an "Ask a Librarian" discussion forum from a course offered in Moodle

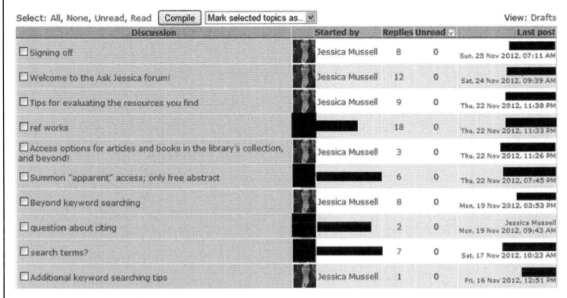

ded in the same course over and over again. Creating a knowledge base helps make the service scalable and sustainable in the long run.

Have librarians follow up with instructors after being embedded to garner feedback on the service. This can be done informally via a quick chat or formally using a survey tool. Consider surveying students as well if you can get permission. Having such data can inform changes and improvements to the structure of the service going forward.

While this recipe was created for libraries with a small complement of librarians, it could just as easily be implemented in larger libraries.

ating resources, as well as a "signing off" post that will provide students with research help contact information after you have left the course.

3. Keep the conversation going. Incorporate a new post each morning on the themes you notice emerging from the previous day's discussions.

ALLERGY WARNINGS
In order for any embedded librarian service to succeed, you need to have buy-in from librarians, faculty, and instructional designers. Outreach to all parties involved, and education around the benefits of this service is critical to your program's success and must be done in advance of launching the service. If offering an entire service seems daunting, try piloting it with a few library-friendly in-

structors, and use the outcomes and feedback from these experiences to promote the service to others.

CHEF'S NOTE
Since implementing the embedded librarian service over a year ago, using this selective process, we have been able to staff embedded librarian requests without impinging too much on librarian workload, even with our small librarian complement (which, if you are wondering, consists of 3 full-time librarians for 2,000 FTE).

Building up a collection of previously written embedded librarian posts that all librarians can share or re-purpose, will make subsequent embedding sessions less time-intensive, particularly if you expect to be embed-